Imperial German Army Motorised Troops 1914-18 Volume 1

Origins, Organization and Mechanical Innovations in the Great War

Jacek Zabielski

Helion & Company Limited
Unit 8 Amherst Business Centre
Budbrooke Road
Warwick
CV34 5WE
England
Tel. 01926 499619
Email: info@helion.co.uk
Website: www.helion.co.uk
X (formerly Twitter): @Helionbooks
Facebook: @HelionBooks
Visit our blog at helionbooks.wordpress.com

Published by Helion & Company 2025
Designed and typeset by Mach 3 Solutions (www.mach3solutions.co.uk)
Cover designed by Paul Hewitt, Battlefield Design (www.battlefield-design.co.uk)

ISBN 978-1-804517-64-2

British Library Cataloguing-in-Publication Data.
A catalogue record for this book is available from the British Library.

Contents

Glossary

Since the author relied on several German-language sources, it might be prudent to outline the approach to translating and naming German units and vehicle types.

The German formation titles are given their full designation upon the first introduction, with no effort made to produce a German-English hybrid. Thus, for example, the 1st Armoured Motor Machine Gun Platoon is initially rendered as the *Panzer Kraftwagen Maschinengewehr Zug-1 / Pz.Kw.MG.Zug-1* or shortly the 1st Platoon / *Zug 1*.

Ordinal numbers are rendered by using a period in German; thus, the 1st Infantry Division is *1.Infanterie Division* (or, for brevity *1.Inf.Div.*) while the 2nd Tank Assault Detachment is *Sturm Panzer Kraftwagen Abteilung 2,* abbreviated as *Sturm Pz. Abt.* 2 or just *Stuka 2*.

Subordinate units within formations are indicated by Arabic numerals for company-size formations (*1, 2,* etc.) and Roman numerals (e.g. *I, II*) for battalions (*Abteilungen*). The term *Abteilung (Abt.)* is generally translated as 'battalion' when it refers to a combat formation or as 'detachment' when it refers to smaller than battalion units representing a specific branch of arms, e.g. assault tank detachment.

Generally, division and higher commands are indicated by ordinal numbers; regiments, battalions, and separate/independent companies typically have the numerical designator following the unit designator.

When the word 'formation' is used, it refers to a battalion or higher element. The term 'unit' is reserved for company-size elements and smaller. Although the term *Schwadron* is literally translated as 'squadron,' this is actually a troop or company in U.S./U.K. usage.

When the original German terminology is unclear, or a mixture of formations and units is being described, then the term 'elements' is used. The spelling *Truppe* is used for 'troops' in the sense of a whole branch or category, and *Truppen* for a number of individuals.

Throughout this text, italics is used for German terms or names, except Panzer - 'armour', and thus, by extension 'tank' - because of its frequent appearance and familiarity to English-speaking readers.

German vehicle types are consistently presented with their full original designations when first introduced, without any attempt to create a German-English hybrid term. This approach maintains the authenticity and precision of the original terminology, ensuring that readers are acquainted with the exact names used by the German military during the period in question. For instance, the term artillery prime mover is accurately referred to as *Artillerie-Kraftzugmaschine*, while the artillery steam engine tractor is designated as *Dampfzugmaschine*, reflecting the specific terminology.

Given the richness of the text in non-English phrases and technical terms, a special section dedicated to abbreviations has been included at the end of this section.

Photos, images and graphics

This book relies on photographs sourced from a variety of public and private collections, including authors collection of postcards (*postkarten*) and photos (AC), Archiv Axel Oskar Mathieu (AAOM), Bayer Hauptstaatsarchiv (BH), Bundesarchiv Koblenz (BK), Imperial War Museum (IWM), Musée des Deux Guerres Mondiales (BDIC), National Archives and Record Administration (NARA), Patton Museum (PM), RAC Tank Museum (RAC TM), and Stuttgart Hauptstaatsarchiv (SH). All org-charts were drafted by the author.

Geographical names

All geographical names, including names of towns, villages, rivers, mountains and mountain ranges, are given in their original form from 1914-18, but where appropriate, the current geographical names have been placed next to the historical names (e.g. Yuryev/ Dorpat, nowadays Tartu).

Linear measurements

Distances and dimensions are given in the metric system of centimetres, meters, and kilometres. Gun calibres below 2cm are specified in millimetres (e.g., 7.92mm), while those above 2cm are listed in centimetres (e.g., 8.0cm).

Abbreviations used in text

Abbr.	***German***	**English**
Abt.	*Abteilung*	Battalion (Bn.) or Detachment (Det.)
	Armee	Field Army
AK	*Armeekorps*	Army Corps
AKD	*Allgemeines Kriegsdepartement*	General War Department
AKK	*Armee-Kraftwagen-Kolonne*	Army Motor Vehicle (MV) Column
AKP	*Armee-Kraftwagen-Park*	Field Army MV Park
AKS	*Armee-Kraftwagen-Staffeln*	Army MV Squadrons
AOK	*Armeeoberkommando*	Army Command
APK	*Artillerie-Prüfungs-Kommission*	Artillery Test Commission
Art.	*Artillerie*	Artillery
Bn.	*Bataillon*	Battalion
Chefkraft	*Chef des Feldkraftfahrwesens*	Chief of Field Motor Vehicles
Div.	*Division*	Division
DKK	*Divisions-Kraftwagen-Kolonne*	Division MV Column
	Etappen	Field Army Rear Echelon / Sector
	Etappen Inspektion	Rear Echelon Transport Inspections
EKK	*Etappen-Kraftwagen-Kolonne*	Rear Echelon MV Column
EKP	*Etappen-Kraftwagen-Park*	Rear Echelon MV Park
ESKA	*Etappen-Sanitäts-Kraftfahrzeug-Abteilung*	Rear Echelon Mot. Ambulance Det.
	Feldartillerie Regimenter auf Kraftwagen	Field Artillery Regt. (mot.)
FAA	*Feld Flieger Abteilung*	Field Flier Detachment
	Feldkraftfahrwesen	Mechanical Transport Service
FKK	*Feldpost-Kraftwagen-Kolonne*	Fieldpost MV Column
FKP	*Festungs-Kraftwagen-Park*	Fortress MV Park
FKA	*Fleisch-Kraftwagen-Kolonne*	Fresch Meat (foodstuff) MV Column
Flak	*Flugabwehrkanone*	Anti-aircraft gun
FKP	*Fussartillerie-Kraftzug-Park*	Foot (Heavy) Art. MV Park
FMK	*Fussartillerie-Munitions-Kolonne*	Foot (Heavy) Art. Ammunition Column
G/Gesch.	*Geschütz*	gun (canon)
	Heeresartillerie Regiment	Independent (reserve) Art. Regt.
Hgr	*Heeresgruppe*	Army Group
	Heimatheer	Home Army
JKD	*Immobiles-Kraftwagen-Depot*	Stationary MV Depot
Ikraft	*Inspektion des Kraftfahrwesens*	Motor Vehicle Inspection
Jasta	*Jagdstaffel*	Fighter Squadron
	Kommandeur der Kraftfahrtruppen	Field CO of Motorized Troops
	Korps	Corps
KKK	*Korps-Kraftwagen-Kolonne*	Corps MV Column
	Kraftfahr-Bataillon	MV Transport Battalion
	Kraftfahr-Kolonne	MV Transport Column
	Kraftfahrtruppe	Motorized (Transport) Troops
	Kraftwagen-Park	Motor Vehicles Depot
K-flak	*Kraftwagenflak*	AA motor vehicle
KK	*Kraftwagen-Kolonne*	motorized column (MC)
KM	*Kriegsministerium*	Ministry of War

Abbr.	*German*	English
MG	*Maschinengewehr*	machine gun
MK	*Militär Kraftwagen*	military motor vehicle
OHL	*Oberste Heeresleitung*	Army High Command
	Panzerkraftwagen-Maschinengewehr-Abt.	Armoured Motor Machine Gun Det.
	Panzerkraftwagen-Maschinengewehr-Zug	Armoured Motor Machine Gun Platoon
SKA / Sanka	*Sanitäts Kraftwagen Abteilung*	Medical Motorized Detachment
Sturm Pz. Abt.	*Sturm-Panzer-Kraftwagen-Abteilung*	Assault Tank Detachment
	Schwere-Kampfwagen-Abteilung	Heavy Assault Tank Detachment
	Staffel	Squadron
	Verkehrstruppen	technical troops
VPK	*Verkehrstechnische-Prüfungs-Kommission*	Evaluation Commission for Transport Technology
	Zug	Platoon
	Zug	prime mover (vehicle)

German motorized transport service soldiers (*Krafthahrtruppen*) clad in pre-war attire stand side by side. The man on the left sports a customary leather jacket (*Lederlitewka*), a leather cap (*Ledermütze*), and goggles, with car badges adorning his collar, denoting his role as a driver. The man on the right dons a parade dress (*Waffenrock* - a dark blue blouse with a black collar, black Swedish cuffs, silver buttons, and black trousers). The light grey shoulder straps indicate rank and the distinct unit number. Both soldiers are equipped with Mauser K.98 rifles. (Photo: Author's collection / AC)

Introduction

The story of the Imperial German Motorized Troops examines the evolution of one of the most pivotal yet often overlooked aspects of the German military during the First World War. This book, and its second volume, meticulously covers the organizational development of the motorized troops (*Kraftfahrtruppen*), tracing their transformation from rudimentary motorized units into more sophisticated and specialized formations by the war's end. The narrative explores the structural changes within these units and also provides a comprehensive examination of the equipment and weaponry that they employed. It provides detailed accounts of the vehicles that were at the forefront of this technological evolution, from the early, experimental vehicles to the few but significant tank designs that emerged from the German war effort. Each chapter highlights how these innovations were born out of necessity and how they were integrated into the broader strategy of the Imperial Army. In addition to the organizational and technical aspects, the book looks at the combat operations of these motorized troops. Through vivid descriptions of key battles and campaigns, readers will gain an understanding of how these units were deployed, the challenges they faced on the battlefield, and their overall impact on the war's outcome. The analysis examines the successes and shortcomings of the German motorized forces, offering insights into why they were ultimately unable to achieve their full potential during the conflict.

What sets this work apart is its rich visual documentation. The book is highly illustrated with many rarely published archive photos, offering a unique visual narrative that complements the text. These images provide an intimate look at the men, machines, and moments that defined the German motorized troops during the Great War. From the dusty roads of the Eastern Front to the muddy trenches of the Western Front, these photographs bring to life the reality of motorized warfare in a way that words alone cannot.

Whether you're a military historian, an enthusiast of early 20th century warfare, or simply curious about the technological and strategic developments of the time, I trust that this book offers a thorough and compelling exploration of a critical, yet underappreciated, chapter in military history.

1
Origins of Military Mechanical Transport

Since ancient times, the mobility of armed forces has been dictated by the movement of infantry alongside horse-drawn wagons. However, a significant shift occurred in the mid-19th century with the introduction of railways, which revolutionized military logistics and mobility. The Prussian Empire's army was particularly forward-thinking in recognizing the potential of mechanized traction. Already during the Schleswig-Holstein Campaigns of 1849-51, they successfully utilized railways for large-scale troop movements, setting a precedent for future military operations.

Building on these early successes, the Prussian General Staff took the innovative step of establishing specialized transportation forces known as *Verkehrstruppen*. These units were responsible for managing and operating the railways, ensuring that troops, equipment, and supplies could be moved swiftly and efficiently to where they were needed most. The *Verkehrstruppen* first saw combat in the Second Schleswig War of 1864 and later played a crucial role in the Austro-Prussian War of 1866.

Initially, these transportation forces were small, mobile units capable of constructing and operating railways close to the front lines. The success of these early efforts not only highlighted the strategic value of railways in warfare but also laid the groundwork for further innovations in military transportation, including the eventual development of motorized and mechanized forces.

During the Franco-German War of 1870-71, the Prussian military continued to innovate in the realm of logistics and transportation, recognizing the critical role that efficient communication and supply lines played in warfare. To enhance these capabilities, a specialized detachment for field railway and telegraph service (*Feldeisenbahn- und Telegraphendienst*) was formed within the elite Guard Pioneer Battalion. This unit was responsible for maintaining and operating the essential infrastructure that connected the front lines with supply depots, ensuring that the Prussian forces could move quickly and maintain effective communication across vast distances.

One of the most notable technological advancements during this conflict was the use of mechanical traction engines, marking their first deployment under actual war conditions. During the Siege of Paris in 1870, Fowler steam road locomotives, which had been ordered by the Prussian Ministry of War (*Kriegsministerium / KM*) in 1869, were pressed into service to support the army's logistical needs. The first two locomotives were delivered on 20 August 1870, and were immediately put to use for general haulage work, demonstrating the potential of steam-powered vehicles in a military context.

Steam road locomotives
Fowler road locomotive in maneuver as a traction engine and power generator during shooting exercises in 1902. (Photo: Archiv Axel Oskar Mathieu / AAOM)

Street locomotive Type A, compound transports railway material near Berlin in 1903. (AAOM).
The newer models of Fowler locomotives, due to their low water and coal consumption, were designed with a triple expansion of steam pressure, which allowed for longer intervals between refueling. These machines weighed 7 tons and were able to pull an average load of 10 tons. Under these conditions, they were able to cover occasional practice marches of 48 km without stopping, at a maximum speed of 6.2km/h.

Freibahnzug tested by the military during the subsidy trip in 1907. (AAOM)

Steam road locomotives
The Prussian army obtained its first road mechanized vehicle / road locomotive from British company Fowler. The machine was a single-cylinder and named Type No.1 Malta in recognition of its origin (first user being British garrison on the island of Malta). The locomotive was capable of carrying a payload of 8 tons, which was distributed on two wagons. It could burn through about 300 kg of coal in a 10-hour workday. (AC)
A Prussian military road locomotive pulling trailers with a horse feed. This particular photo was probably taken in 1914, but similar road trains were first used as early as 1870 during the Prussian-French War. (AC)

Fowler Maltas were utilized by the Berlin-based *Verkehrstruppen* from 1901.
The term *Verkehrstruppen* referred to a military branch specializing in telephony, radio communication, and field aeronautics. The *Verkehrstruppen* also encompassed units involved in operations utilizing railways, motor (steam and bezel) vehicles and bicycles. (AC)

These *Fowler* steam locomotives, however, were not purpose-built for military operations. They were standard commercial models, not specially modified for the rigors of war. Despite this, they proved effective in their role, showcasing the versatility and power of mechanical traction. Each of these locomotives weighed approximately 40 tons and generated around 20 horsepower (hp), a substantial amount of power for the time. Their ability to transport heavy loads over rough terrain provided the Prussian army with a logistical edge, allowing them to sustain the siege and maintain pressure on Paris.

Within their first five days of service, road locomotives transported a dozen store wagons over 45 kilometers from Pont-a-Mousson to Commercy. Subsequently, they transported ammunition and coal between Nanteuil and Villeneuve St. Georges over seven days, aiding the German supply route threatened by the destruction of the Nanteuil railway tunnel.

Following the lessons learned in the Franco-Prussian War, the first railway battalion was established, later supplemented by a second battalion in 1876, eventually forming the first Railway Regiment (*Eisenbahnregiment*).

The final organizational structure of this new logistical and technical formation was solidified on 25 March 1899, with the establishment of the Inspectorate of Transport Troops (*Inspektion der Verkehrstruppen*) based in Berlin. A few days later, a Motor Vehicle Command (*Selbstfahrer Kommando*) was created, addressing automobile-related matters.

The first attempts to use motorized vehicles for the army's needs occurred already in 1899 during Imperial maneuvers, where several passenger cars and motorcycles were employed for transmitting orders and reports. In the same year, the military department of the German Automobile Club (*Deutsche- Automobil-Club / DAC*) was founded, expressing its willingness to adapt its vehicles to the army's needs and to potential wartime requirements. This initiative granted its members the status of reserve officers. On 24 December 1905, *Kaiser* Wilhelm II personally assumed patronage of the *DAC*, prompting a name change to Imperial Automobile Club (*Kaiserlicher-Automobil-Club / KAC*).

During the military maneuvers in 1904, 22 cars and 34 motorcycles were deployed, and within five years, this number increased to around 100 passenger cars and a similar quantity of motorcycles. Consequently, the Army High Command (*Oberste Heeresleitung / OHL*) initiated preparations to mobilize civilian vehicles in case of war, leading to the issuance of relevant ordinances in 1905, 1909, and 1912.

In 1902, the Prussian War Ministry and the Ministry for Agriculture announced a reward for a truck capable of cross-country transportation of a 10 ton load with two trailers. Responding to this challenge Daimler and NAG truck manufacturers offered conventional tractors, while Siemens introduced a novel concept of a tractor featuring four wheels of 2m diameter, all driven by electric motors in their hubs, powered by a gasoline-driven generator. This vehicle, featuring two independently moving halves, represented an early example of articulated drive. In 1906, Siemens received an order from the army for a similar but simpler road train capable of transporting 15 tons on five trailers, all driven by an electric engine on the rear axle. However, these road trains proved detrimental to roads and exhibited poor off-road capability, resulting in their final rejection by the Imperial Army.

Despite proposals in 1907 by General Richter for combat motor vehicles, such as field guns with armor shields accompanying infantry, and Burstyn's 1912 suggestion for a motorized armored gun on tracks, these ideas went unheeded.

The Imperial crown symbol is displayed on the passenger cabin doors, in addition to the Kaiserlicher Automobil Club (KAC) emblem on the driver's doors, including an enlarged version of the *KAC* symbol in its original colors (AC)

The Imperial German Automobile Club
The *Kaiserlicher Automobil Club* (*KAC*) existed in Germany since 1899 and was instrumental in several pioneering efforts to raise automotive standards, including introducing the first automobile liability law. It is estimated that in 1911, the *KAC* had about 17,000 members, among them more than 12,000 car owners. The *KAC* members' cars were marked with a special badge, which consisted of a gilded bronze circle (15 cm) enameled in white containing the Prussian Imperial eagle within a shield, surrounded by the Gothic letters *KAC* and underneath the German crown. Some badges had a cartouche on the bottom with the membership number painted.
Pre-war vehicles marked with the *KAC* badge. (AC)

Pre-war military trucks and cars
In 1905, Daimler developed a new truck model, which, with its honeycomb radiator, visually resembled the Mercedes. (AAOM)

Two Adlers type L.S. 4/40 with trailers in the Taunu Mountains in 1912. This type was developed with state financial assistance of the Imperial German Army. (AAOM)

While the Ministry of War endeavored to support production efforts for heavy lorries through subsidies, garrisons autonomously acquired staff cars. These vehicles served primarily as tools for senior officers in commanding and controlling operations. (AAOM)
A staff car belonging to an air service detachment based in the garrison (fortress) of Graudenz (nowadays Grudziądz, Poland) in 1913. The car is decorated with a homemade plate with *Nach Mutteren* (To Mother) inscription. (AC)

1.1 Laying the organizational foundations

A pivotal step in the motorization of the Prussian army occurred in April 1907 with the establishment of the Motor Vehicles Detachment (*Kraftfahre-Abteilung*) at Tempelhof Airfield, which was based on the Prussian Motor Vehicle Command (*Selbstfahrer Kommando*) established in 1899. This detachment, comprising a 150-man-strong company, served as the training and experimental unit, primarily focused on the utilization of trucks for transport and supplies.

The organizational changes also took place within the Ministry of War, specifically in General War Department (*Allgemeines Kriegsdepartement / AKD*) where the Section 7 known as *Abteilung 7 Verkehrstruppen* (*A7V*) was established. This section was assigned critical responsibilities related to military motor vehicles, including specifications and procurement, trials, testing and development of special army trucks with trailers, which could transport up to 6 tons of cargo at speeds ranging from 8 to 12 kilometers per hour. Given the limited road infrastructure of the time, this capability was impressive and contributed substantially to the army's logistical efficiency.

The procurement and testing procedures were also under the oversight of the Evaluation Commission for Transport Technology (*Verkehrstechnische-Prüfungs-Kommission / VPK*) and Artillery Test Commission (*Artillerie-Prüfungs-Kommission / APK*), especially regarding the mechanical traction considerations for heavy (called in German army - foot) artillery.

The *APK* initially focused on steam-powered vehicles, featuring robust road engines with 41 and 53 horsepower, capable of towing loads of 18 and 24 tons, respectively, at speeds ranging from 5 to 7 kilometers per hour. Steam power was also applied to transport loads such as the 42cm *Gamma-Mortar* or the 15cm *Kanone in Schirmlafette*, as well as the heavy guns of Metz fortress. These guns were planned to be moved between positions either by road transport (short-distance) or railway (long-distance), sitting on steel trailers.

While the War Ministry was still hesitant about the concept of motorized combat vehicles, it expressed interest in the mobile guns designed for pursuing balloons and dirigibles (*Ballonabwehrkanonen / BAK*). This led to the makeshift solution of producing around 150 four-ton trucks with mounted 5.7cm guns before 1914.

1.2 State subsidies

The German War Ministry was among the pioneers in implementing a war subsidy (or subvention) to finance a reserve of road vehicles that the army could quickly mobilize in the event of hostilities. Initially, the requirements were informal, and by 1907, only approximately 158 assorted lorries had been registered for subsidies.

In 1908, specific regulations were established for vehicles eligible for subsidies. The maximum permitted weight was set at 4.5 tons with a 4 ton payload, with the gross weight not exceeding 9 tons (from 1909 an additional 2 tons trailer was requested). The power should not be less than 35 horsepower. Each lorry had to be equipped with a trailer, and both the lorry and the trailer had to have dimensions less than 2 meters wide, with a track width of no more than 150cm. These stringent width restrictions, resulting in very narrow vehicles, were intentionally chosen to optimize the vehicle for use on French (rather than German) roads.

Pre-war trucks and lorries
A heavy commercial lorry (NAG 1910, 5 tones) mobilized in 1914. The vehicle is still in the pre-war, bright color but is already marked with the Prussian coat of arms. (AC)

The NAG factory, or *Neue Automobil Gesellschaft*, established in 1902, began producing army-subsidized lorries in 1910. The photo depicts one of its first military models (*Armee-Lastzug*) produced under introduced in 1910. (AAOM)

Another *NAG Type 1913*, subsidized by the Army starting in 1912. (AAOM)

The subsidy amounted to 4,000 Marks, along with a four-year maintenance premium to support the vehicle's cost and upkeep. These funds were made available to all individuals and companies purchasing a vehicle suitable for the army. In return, the buyers committed to making their vehicles available to the army in the event of mobilization. The first subsidy trials under this program took place in the summer of 1909.

This funding approach not only helped minimize acquisition costs but also addressed the negative social sentiments surrounding the early use of mechanical vehicles. This was particularly significant since, at the beginning of the 20th century, cars and lorries elicited various unfavorable reactions due to factors such as noise, the perceived risk of road accidents, and even the potential for explosions. The military aimed to redirect the aversion associated with owning these 'hell machines' towards civilians rather than the army. Another method employed to manage aversion was painting vehicles in bright red to diminish the risk of unexpected encounters between pedestrians and cars. This practice was implemented on numerous civilian and possibly some military vehicles.

The subsidy program achieved limited success, with only 743 subsidized trucks available to the Prussian Army between 1908 and 1912, and an additional 82 trucks allocated to the Bavarian Army. The situation was even more dire for passenger cars, as no funds had been allocated for military-grade field cars or even suitable staff vehicles.

Within its own procurement, the army predominantly acquired specialized vehicles designed for heavy artillery (tractors) batteries, air detachments, or mobile ambulances for garrison hospitals (*Krankenkraftwagen*).

1.3 Initial order of battle

By 1912, the German automobile industry was already manufacturing approximately 30,000 vehicles annually, contributing to a total vehicle count of 70,000 (93,072 in 1914 of which 60,876 were passenger cars, 9,639 trucks and 22,557 motorcycles). About 10 percent of these were lorries designated for potential use by the army transport troops in the event of war, mostly by the so-called Rear Echelon Motorized Vehicle Columns (*Etappen-Kraftwagen-Kolonnen / EKK*). While the total number of trucks was on the rise, the growth rate for subsidized (military-optimized) trucks was considerably less dynamic. At the outset of 1913, only 825 such trucks were in operation across various businesses, with breweries dominating at 43 percent, followed by the transport sector at 23 percent, and brickmakers, mills, and farmers.

The mobilization plans outlined in 1909 stipulated that each Field Army (*Armee*) would have one Motor Vehicles Park / Depot (*Etappen-Kraftwagen-Park / EKP*), multiple transport columns (*EKK)*, and one Stationary Motorized Vehicles Depot/Park (*Immobile-Kraftwagen-Depot / JKD*). A year later, the plans underwent revision, envisioning the establishment of eight Transport Troops Commands (*Kommandeur der Kraftfahrtruppen*), 27 transport columns, and eight car parks in the event of war.

Motor vehicles were also designated for heavy artillery units and motorized anti-aircraft artillery units. The latter saw the introduction of the first AA mobile guns as early as 1905 (5.0cm caliber), and in 1909, the range expanded with 7.5cm caliber guns mounted on a truck chassis.

Pre-war trucks and lorries
The Imperial German Army employed a Siemens gasoline-electric road locomotive with electrically driven trailers from (?) 1905 to 1910. (AAOM)

A Daimler-Siemens petrol-electric road locomotive, model 1908, was capable of pulling up to four heavy trailers. (Photo: Reed Büssing Info)

An Ansbach lorry with the trailer from the Bavarian Royal Railway Battalion (*Königlichen Eisenbahnbataillons*) in Munich prepared for the field maneuvers in 1909. (AAOM)

In 1900, the Daimler-Motoren-Gesellschaft was established, which from 1902, manufactured passenger cars under the brand name Mercedes. Additionally, the company produced commercial vehicles such as trucks and lorries under the brand name *Daimler*. Among these was one of the pioneering heavy lorries designed and delivered in 1906 for the Experimental Detachment of Transport Troops (*Versuchs Abteilung der Verkehrstruppen*). (AAOM)

A NAG lorry, model 1910, with its front axle broken due to the extremely bad East Prussian road surfaces. Note the censored (all-white) license plate. This heavy vehicle was most likely registered to Provinz Brandenburg. (AC)

As already mentioned, the Imperial Army overlooked the development of armored fighting vehicles despite testing three prototypes armed with machine guns in 1909. The Inspectorate of Transport Troops decided to discontinue these tests due to limited usefulness.

In 1908, the Bavarian Army, independently of the Prussians, established its own Motor Transport Battalion within the Railroad Battalion. Eventually, on 1 October 1911, it was integrated into the Balloon Detachment, renamed as *Luft-und Kraftfahr-Abteilung* (Air and Motor Transport Battalion). This formation comprised three companies, including a Saxon section in the 2nd Coy and a Wurttemberg section in the 3rd Coy. A fourth company was added two years later, on 1 October 1913, increasing its personnel strength to 735 troops.

Despite the rapid advancements in motorized transport at the dawn of the 20th century, these innovations were still largely in their infancy on the eve of the First World War. As a result, motorized transport formations continued to occupy a secondary, supportive role.

At that time, motorized formations were integrated into what was known as the technical forces, a specialized branch responsible for supporting the broader operational needs of the military. Specifically, they were subordinate to the General Inspector of Communication Forces (*General Inspektion des Militar Verkehrswesens*), an overarching authority tasked with overseeing all aspects of military transportation and logistics.

These technical forces were crucial in coordinating the movement and supply of troops and materials, but their role was often limited to supplementing traditional methods of transportation such as railways and horse-drawn wagons. The motorized units, while promising, had not yet reached the level of integration or operational capacity necessary to take on a primary role in front-line engagements.

The *Verkehrswesens*, which encompassed all branches of military transportation and communication, was the smallest component of the German army in terms of personnel. It included several units, each specializing in different aspects of military logistics and/or support. The main components were:

1. **Inspectorate of Railway Troops** *(Inspektion der Eisenbahntruppen):* this unit managed the railways' military operations, crucial for transporting troops and supplies across vast distances. It consisted of:
   - **1st Railway Brigade (Berlin)**: This brigade included:
     - **Railway Regiment Nos. 1 / 4**
   - **2nd Railway Brigade (Hanau)**: This brigade included:
     - **Railway Regiment Nos. 2 / 3**

2. **Field Telegraphy Inspectorate** *(Inspektion der Feldtelegraphie):* responsible for the establishment and maintenance of field telecommunication systems, which were essential for coordinating movements and operations. It included:
   - **1st Telegraphy Inspectorate (Berlin)**: this inspectorate oversaw:
     - **Telegraph Battalion Nos. 1 / 7 (Saxon)**
   - **2nd Telegraphy Inspectorate (Karlsruhe)**: this inspectorate managed:
     - **Telegraph Battalion Nos. 3/ 4 /6**
   - **3rd Telegraphy Inspectorate (Danzig)**: this inspectorate controlled:
     - **Telegraph Battalion Nos. 2 / 5**

Pre-war trucks and lorries
On 1 October 1911, the first Motor Transport Bn. (*Kraftfahr Bataillon*) was formed in Germany. It consisted of three companies, including a Saxon section in the 2nd company and a Wurttemberg section in the 3rd company.
The lorry (Lloyd 50-52 PS) from the 1st Company (1.Comp.) of the *Kraftfahr Battalion* showcased the battalion's name prominently painted on the tarp and the load box. This photo was captured between 1912/1913. (AC)

Kraftfahr Bataillon, 2.Comp. truck with the handwritten inscription *Heimat* (Homeland) on the load box and the unit name on the tarp. Photo taken between 1912-1913. (AC)

A Dürkopps Kavallerie-Wagen Type L 60 delivered to the *Kraftfahr Bataillion, 4 Compagnie* in 1913. Photo taken in early 1915. (AC)

Pre-war motor vehicles
The photo depicts officers and staff cars from the Motor Transport Bn. (*Kraftfahr Batl.*), specifically, the Rear Echelon/Sector Motorized Detachments (*Kraftfahr-Etappen-Abteilung 8 / EA 8*) used by a driving school (*Fahrschule*) affiliated with the VI. (Home) Army Corps. (Photo: Vestes Bellica)

A Büssing lorry from the *Kraftfahr Bn.*, photographed in Berlin in the summer of (?)1912. The truck had right-hand steering, as was usual in that era even for German vehicles. If this is indeed 1912 than it proves that the Imperial eagle (*Reichadler*) symbol was occasionally used before the outbreak of the First World War. (AC)

A Hansa-Lloyd truck was developed with state subsidies prior to the Great War. This specific vehicle belonged to the Airship Battalion, 2nd Coy (*Luftschiffer-Batallion 2, 2. Kompagne*). Judging by the *Reichsadler* emblem used to denote the vehicle, the photo was taken in late 1914. (AAOM)

3. **Aviation and Automobile Inspectorate** *(Inspektion des Militar-Luft- und Kraft-Fahrwesens):* this unit was responsible for the development and management of air and motorized transport. It included:
   - **Airship Inspectorate**: Managed:
     - **Airship Battalions Nos. 1-5**
   - **Air Force Inspectorate** *(Inspektion der Fliegertruppen):* responsible for:
     - **Air Battalions Nos. 1-5**

4. **Motor Vehicles Battalion** *(Kraftfahr-Bataillon):* this battalion was part of the Prussian Imperial Guard Corps *(Gardekorps)* and was responsible for managing motor vehicles. It was organized into:
   - **Four Companies**:
     - **A Saxon platoon** formed in the 2nd Company
     - **A Württemberg platoon** in the 3rd Company

In addition, small units of technical troops also served with:

- the Bavarian army, in the **Aviation and Motor Vehicles Battalion** *(Luft und Kraftfahrbataillon)* as well as in two telegraph battalions, and
- the Saxon army (telegraph battalion), and
- the Wurttemberg army, which was later incorporated into the Prussian army.

At this stage, the motor battalions of the Prussian and Bavarian armies, numbering around 1,100 soldiers combined, were the smallest units within the technical formations and minuscule compared to the overall size of the army.

In the event of mobilization, the German military planned to requisition approximately 4,000 vehicles, which included around 1,700 trucks (out of which 800 had been part of the subvention program).

This plan was realized in August 1914, at the outbreak of First World War, when these vehicles were successfully integrated into the army's logistics and transport operations.

Alongside the requisition of civilian trucks, the Motorized Troops underwent a rapid expansion in personnel. The corps grew to include 200 officers and approximately 8,000 to 12,000 non-commissioned officers and enlisted men. While this represented a significant increase from the peacetime strength of the *Kraftfahrtruppe*, it was still a relatively small force when compared to the overall size of the Imperial German Army, which numbered around 800,000 soldiers at the start of the war.

Wartime trucks and lorries

Germany quickly saw the military advantages of the motor vehicle, with the Daimler Phoenix petrol-powered 'motor lorry' making its debut in 1898, the wartime production of German mechanized vehicles was insufficient to meet the demands of the military. Still many models were in use.

A lorry from the 11th Rear Echelon/Sector Motorized Column (*EKK 11*) in the principality of Lüneburg (Brunswick) in 1914. It has a circle 'sign' on the radiator cover made by the fan. (AC)

In 1914, the German automotive industry, was capable of manufacturing around 30,000 vehicles annually, including 1,850 trucks, a substantial output that could be leveraged for military purposes. Starting in 1915, the annual demand for military trucks increased to 10,000 vehicles. By that same year, production peaked, reaching a level of 15,000 cargo trucks.

The army's pre-war motorized transport capability was further supplemented by the Volunteer Automobile Corps (*Freiwilligen Automobil-Korps*), established in 1904 under the auspices of Germany's automobile club. This corps aimed to provide competent drivers and roadworthy motor cars available for military service in times of war. Membership in the *Freiwilligen Automobil-Korps* was by invitation only and restricted to German citizens, all of whom were armed, uniformed, and required to fulfill up to 30 days of paid training annually in peacetime.

A *Benz* lorry from the 31st Rear Echelon/Sector Motorized Column *(EKK 31, V. Armee)*. Western Front 1914. (AC)

Drivers formed into a security detachment guarding vehicles gathered at the 7th Rear Echelon/Sector Motorized Vehicles Depot (*EKP 7 / VII. Armee*). France, 27 October 1915. (AC)

Wartime trucks and lorries
A German military truck damaged at Lagery, located 20 kilometers southwest of Reims, which the Imperial Army captured in early September 1914. Following the intense battle in the area surrounding Reims, it was recaptured by the French on 12-13 September Despite the loss of the city, the Germans held positions on the high ground, periodically shelling Reims over the next four years. (AC)

A German transport column in Roucy, France. The village, except for a few days in September 1914 and a few weeks in the summer of 1918, remained French throughout the Great War. (AC)

Trucks from the *EKK 38 / II.Armee,* 1915, based in Hénin-Liétard, France 1915. (AC)

2
Army Transport Service

2.1 Railway transport

In spite of advancements in pre-war petrol- and steam-powered motor transport, the Imperial Army continued to rely heavily on railway traction. This reliance was evident in the German plan to attack France in 1914, which envisioned a rapid concentration of forces along the western borders through the use of trains. Even upon entering enemy territory, the Germans planned to rely on the Belgian and French railway infrastructure to supply their forces. In reality, after crossing the French border, the rapidly advancing German troops surpassed their supply lines, including the railway. This led to shortages in food and ammunition, compounded by increased resistance from the French, who efficiently utilized their well-developed rail network around Paris and even private taxis to mobilize a new army for the defense of the capital. Consequently, the German advance came to a halt.

Maintaining a vast *static* army in the field demanded substantial supplies, and also at this stage, railways emerged as the key means to transport such vast quantities of materials across the land. A highly sophisticated transportation and supply system was established to facilitate this process. While reaching the vicinity of the front line posed relatively fewer challenges, the real difficulties arose approximately 10 kilometers behind the front. Beyond this point, the threat of devastating long-distance artillery shelling loomed large. Consequently, the establishment of main supply depots and railway yards had to be carried out before entering this perilous zone. Bridging the gap between these supply points and the soldiers in need presented the next challenge.

A 10 kilometers distance proved too extensive for effective transportation using horse-drawn wagons, as horses couldn't manage a daily round trip of such length. The Germans, however, had a solution at hand, having introduced the 60cm gauge light railway system before the war. This system could be easily laid on the ground and relocated as needed.

Over time, horse-drawn wagons and light trains were gradually supplemented with motor vehicles.

Railway transport Wherever rail systems were available, the army logistical services relied heavily upon them to move men, supplies, guns, wagons and also motor vehicles. Cars from the Graudenz (nowadays Grudziądz in Poland) garrison on the way to the front line, likely around 1916. Military vehicles were moved to the front-line rear sector primarily on so-called flatcars. (AC)

Military trucks entrained at the station Wiggoda in West Prussia (now Poland, Wygoda near Kościerzyna) in May 1916. The vehicles are painted in plain Feldgrau, except for the tarpaulins. (AC)

A wheeled artillery tractor *Krupp-Daimler K.D. I* and a 15cm gun entrained at a railway station somewhere in northern France in the autumn of 1918. It seems to be the complete gun section including a staff car. (AC)

Railway transport
The large concentrations of soldiers and artillery in the West demanded the delivery of vast quantities of food, ammunition, and construction materials for fortifications, especially in areas where transport infrastructure had been destroyed. Rebuilding conventional roads, which were often unsurfaced at the time, proved too slow. This issue was addressed by the use of trench (narrow-gauge) railways, which connected the front lines to standard-gauge railway networks beyond the reach of enemy artillery.
Empty railcars of trench railways often carried wounded returning from the front. (AC)

An 11-tonne 0-8-0T *Brigadelok* German locomotive design with *Klien-Lindner* was adopted as the military standard in 1901. Approximately 250 were available by 1914, and over two thousand were produced during the war. A *Brigadelok* typically handled six loaded cars up a 2% grade. (AC)

Soldiers of the Railway Regt. laying narrow-gauge railway tracks in the Ypres Salient. (Photo: Alamy)

2.2 Organization of the Motorized Transport Troops 1914-1918

In the summer of **1914**, out of the total civilian vehicle pool of 93,000, only 4,820 were mobilized, including approximately 1,700 lorries that met the military's requirements. These vehicles were assigned to various motorized detachments, involving around 200 officers and 8,000 to 12,000 soldiers. These personnel were assigned to command staffs and special weapons units within Field Armies (*Armees*) and the Home Army (*Heimatheer*).

Every army-level headquarters (*AOK*) featured a Commander of Motorized Troops (*Kommandeur der Kraftfahrtruppen*) along with a staff comprising five officers and 27 other ranks within an Inspectorate of the Rear-Army Sector (*Etappen Inspektion*) responsible for an area behind the front line up to the Imperial, national border).

This headquarters staff oversaw the transport activities of vehicles in:

Rear-Echelon Motorized Vehicles (MV) Columns (*Etappen-Kraftwagen-Kolonnen / EKK*)
truck columns of cavalry units (*Kavallerie-Lastkraftwagen-Kolonnen / KKK*),
motor ambulance formations (*Sanitäts-Kraftfahrformationen / SKK*) subdivided into
– truck/transport columns (*Lastkraftwagen-Kolonne*), and
– ambulance columns (*Krankenkraftwagen-Kolonne*)
both subordinated to Rear-Echelon Medical Depots (*Etappensanitätsdepots*),
Rear-Echelon (MV) Parks (*Etappen-Kraftwagen-Park / EKP*), and
MV Fortification Parks (*Kraftwagenparks in Festungen*).

The allocation of transport columns or *EKK's* in 1914 for each *Armee* was contingent on the distance it needed to cover during the execution of the Field Marshal Schlieffen offensive. The *I* and *II. Armees* were assigned 18 *EKK's, III - 9, IV & V - each 5, VI - 8, VII - 3, VIII - 0.* Additionally, each cavalry division had its column known as *Kavellerie KK* (*11*), and all active *Jäger Battalions* had one (16 *KK*).

The transport columns varied in size from company to platoon, undertaking the transportation of equipment, a fixed cargo of supplies, or even light infantry.

The *Inspektorate* held responsibility for various units, including the Motor Vehicles Squadron with cars and lorries (*Kraftwagen-Staffelen*), the Motorcycle Detachment (*Kraftradfahrer-Abteilung*), and the Rear-Echelon Mot. Ambulance Detachment (*Etappen-Sanitäts-Kraftfahrzeug-Abteilung*). The *Inspektorate* also received support from the *Allgemeinen-Deutschen-Automobil-Korps*, utilized for transporting voluntary medical care (*Freiwilligen Krankenpfleger*) which consisted of civilians who were provided to the medical corps and the wounded as directed by the *Etappenarzt* (Rear-Echelon Chief Doctor).

A distinct vehicle pool was designated for the Foot/Heavy Artillery (*Fussartillerie*), consisting of 3 Road Locomotives (powered by steam engines) Parks (*Dampfpflug-Lokomotiv-Parks*) and 2 Artillery Tractors (powered by benzol engines) Columns (*Benzoltraktoren-Kolonnen*).

In September 1914, each *Armeekorps* acquired new combustion engine-powered vehicles, forming the Fresh Meat Motorized Columns (*Fleisch-Kraftwagen-Kolonne*) used for transportation of strategic perishable resources.

During the autumn of 1914, eight-vehicle-strong field post transportation columns (*Fieldpost-Kraftwagen-Kolonnen*) were established to handle mail transportation. Separate detachments were created for the Imperial Prussian (*Keiserlich-Deutschen-Feldpost*), Bavarian (*Bayerishen Feldpost*), and Wurttemberg military post service.

In March **1915**, General Quartiermeister issued orders to standardize motorized transport units. The cavalry and light infantry (*Jäger*), with a few exceptions, lost their transport columns, which were transferred to the Rear-Army Sectors (*Etappen*).

Simultaneously, Divisions not affiliated with a Corps received a *Divisions-Kraftwagen-Kolonne*.

Wartime cars, trucks and lorries During the invasion of Belgium in 1914, the German Army was afraid of irregular forces known as *Francs-tireurs*. The marching soldiers were vulnerable to these attacks, but officers in staff cars attempted to protect themselves by fitting them with a device called a *Kabelschneider*. The purpose of the device was to cut or deflect barbed wire strung across the road. The number of cars equipped with the *Kabelschneider* remained relatively low, as the modification was improvised. (AC)

A lorry from the 8th Light Infantry Bn., Bicycle Coy (*Jäg. Batl. 8 Rafd. Komp.*). The mobile light infantry units were attached in 1914 to Cavalry Divisions. As the war progressed, many new bicycle units were raised, bringing the total number to 80 companies by 1918. (AC)

A column from the Bavarian Air and Motor Bn. (*Bayer. Luft- u. Kraftfahrer-Bataillon*) halt for a photo near Strasbourg in 1914. The first car seems to be the *Benz* 10/30PS, the one behind 8/20PS followed by the 8/20 model. All cars are registered to *Festungs* (fortress) *Gouvernement Strassburg*. (AC)

Wartime trucks and lorries

Rare photo of the *EKK 29* vehicles, subordinated to *Etappen Inspektion* from the *II.Armee.* Photos taken in late 1914, somewhere in France. Some vehicles of *EKK 29* were marked with an alphanumeric code painted on the sides (e.g. **L 4** = *Lastkraftwagen* No. 4 / Lorry No. 4). (AC)

The large number on the bonnet (1401) was the individual car registration number (II-1401); while **P5** = *Personenkraftwagen* No. 5 / Staff car No. 5) was used as the type designator. (AC)

A lorry of the 74th Balloon Platoon (*Ballonzug 74*) from the *V.Armee* in front of the Belgian railway station in Roeselare, 1914. Belgium, though neutral, was invaded by Germany as part of the Schlieffen Plan, which aimed to quickly defeat France by advancing through Belgium. (AC)

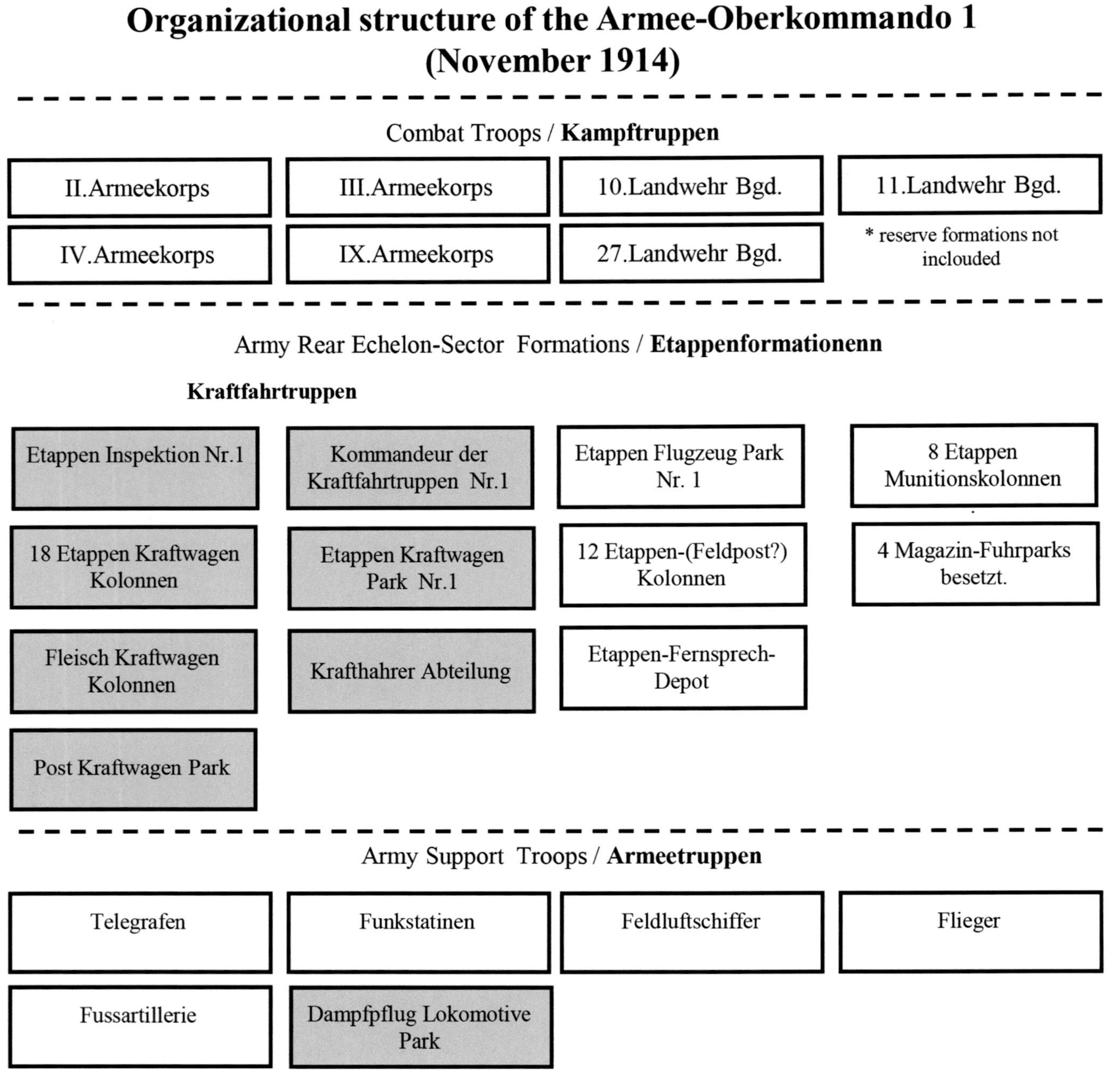

The gray-shaded boxes represent Imperial German Army units that provided various types of motorized transport services, including the transport of ammunition and supplies (Etappen-Kraftwagen-Kolonnen), fresh meat transport (Fleisch-Kraftwagen-Kolonnen), and postal delivery (Post-Kraftwagen-Park), all supervised by the Etappen-Inspektion and the Kommandeur der Kraftfahrtruppen. Additionally, at the Army level, a dedicated detachment (Dampfpflug-Lokomotiven-Park) operated road locomotives used for towing super-heavy siege howitzers.

Organizational structure of *Armee-Oberkommando 1* (November 1914). (AC)

Etappen Kraftwagen Park
Staff cars, trucks and lorries of an unidentified *Armeekorps* in the Western Front in 1915. (AC)

Wartime trucks and lorries
When the war broke out, the German military had approximately 1,500 trucks and lorries at its disposal. This fleet was significantly retrofitted in the first year of the war, and by mid-1915, the number of trucks had already risen to over 10,000.
A Mercedes truck with pennants identifying divisional HQ detachment and non-standard letter code G W (Wagen No. G ?). (AC)

Trucks from an unidentified transport unit photographed near the French town of Cunel, near Verdun, in 1915. (AC)

Trucks belonging to the *XI.Armee* at the Balkan Front (Montenegro) in 1916. Road accidents happened frequently because of bad roads, overstressed vehicle components and tired drivers. (AC)

Key to military symbols

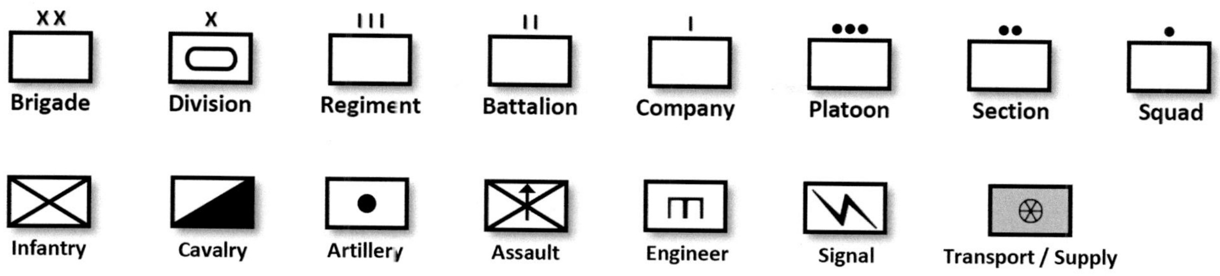

German **Cavalry Divisions**, each composed of three brigades with two regiments per brigade, were designed for operational independence and capable of conducting reconnaissance and combat missions ahead of the main army. Their transport relied primarily on horses but also included a single motorized transport column. Additionally, the Jäger Battalion (light infantry mounted on bicycles) attached to cavalry division prior to the outbreak of the Great War were equipped with trucks.

ORDER OF BATTLE

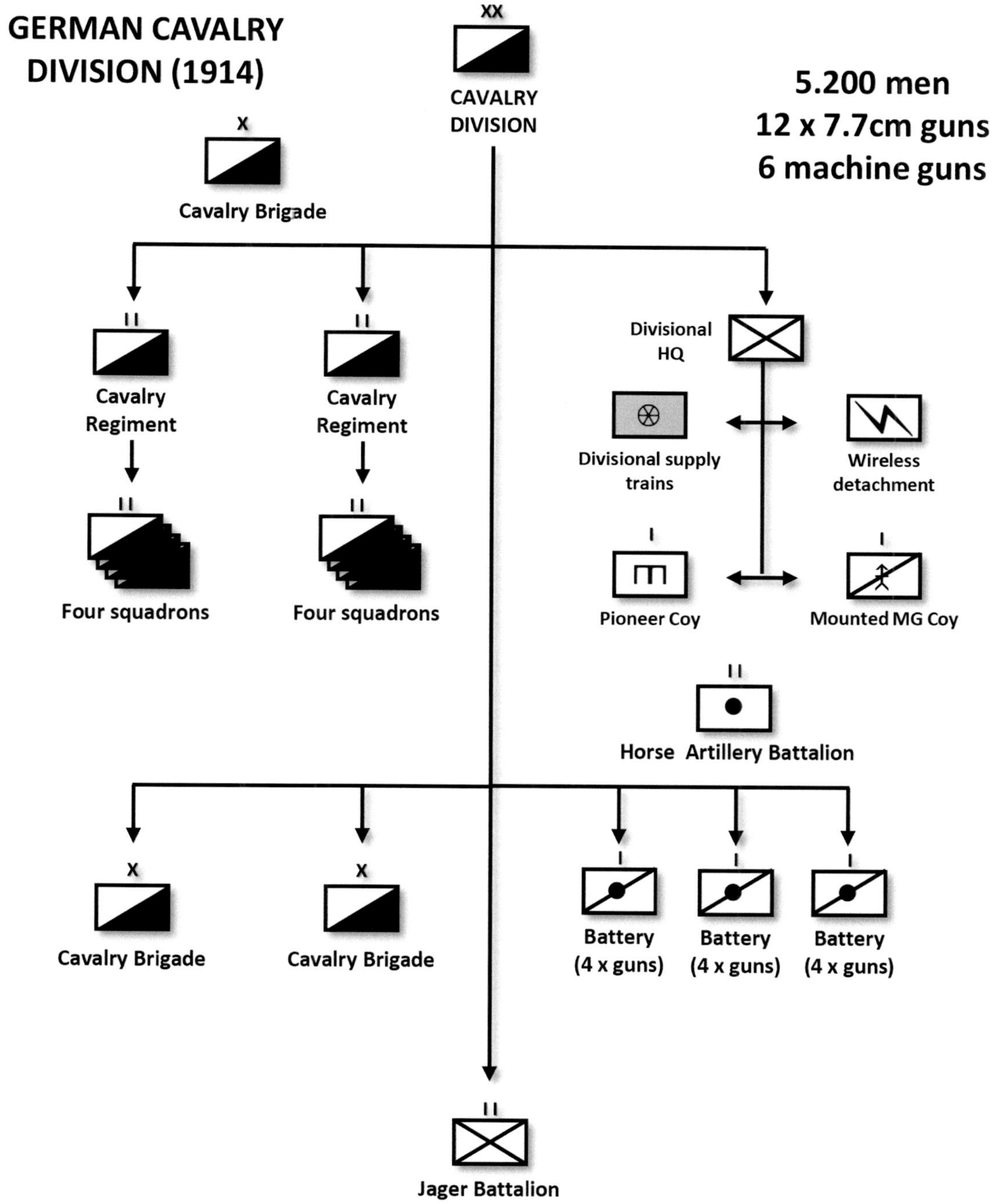

Wartime trucks and lorries
German troops being transported to the Braila front in Romania (1916). Some pioneers could be present on the truck, given the presence of the long shovel. (Photo: Imperial War Museum / IWM)

German lorries from the *III.Armee* in the West, 1916. (AC)

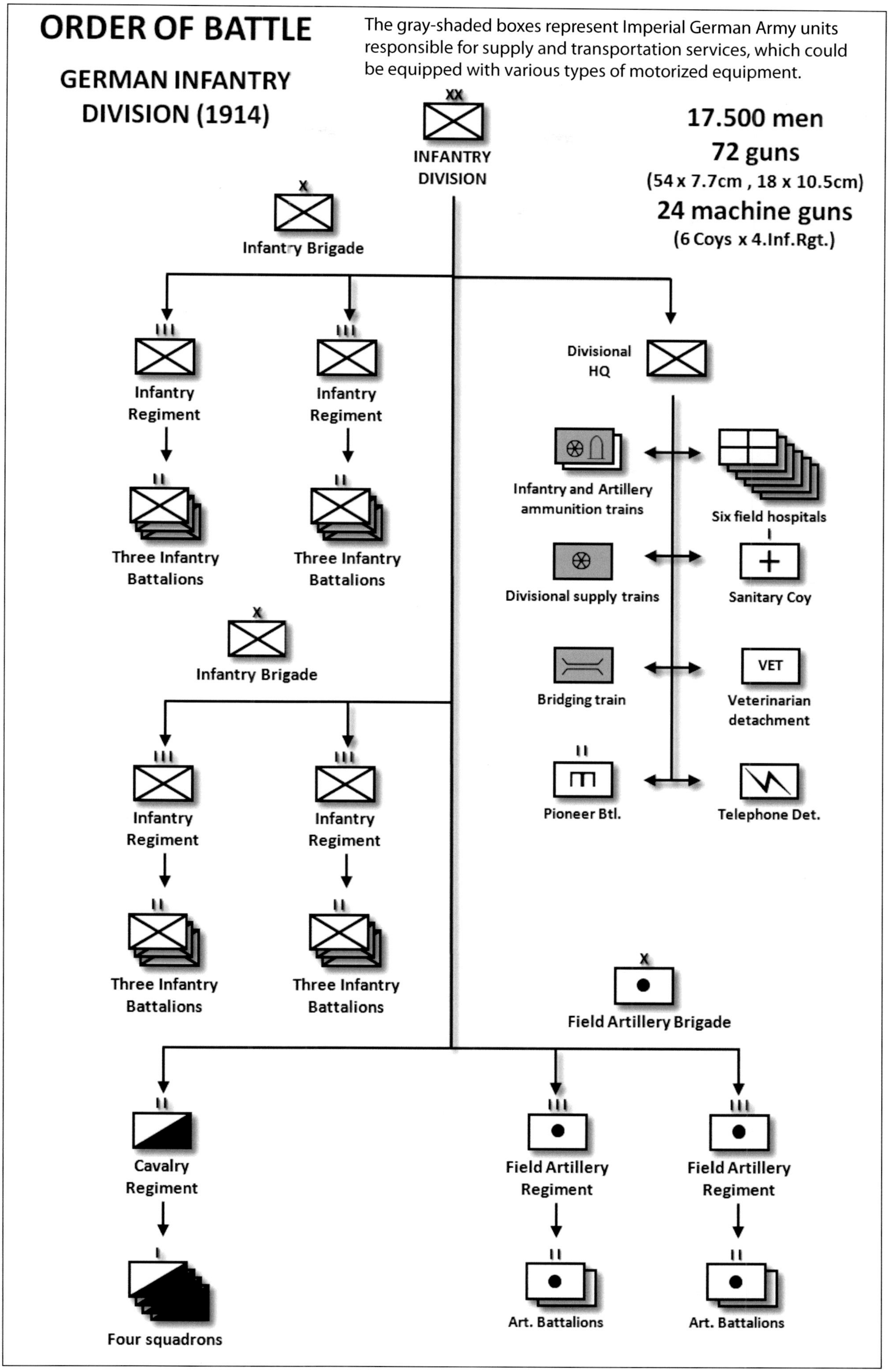
ORDER OF BATTLE
GERMAN INFANTRY DIVISION (1914)
The gray-shaded boxes represent Imperial German Army units responsible for supply and transportation services, which could be equipped with various types of motorized equipment.
XX
INFANTRY DIVISION
17.500 men
72 guns
(54 x 7.7cm , 18 x 10.5cm)
24 machine guns
(6 Coys x 4.Inf.Rgt.)
X
Infantry Brigade
III
Infantry Regiment
II
Three Infantry Battalions
III
Infantry Regiment
II
Three Infantry Battalions
Divisional HQ
Infantry and Artillery ammunition trains
Six field hospitals
Divisional supply trains
I
Sanitary Coy
Bridging train
VET
Veterinarian detachment
II
Pioneer Btl.
Telephone Det.
X
Infantry Brigade
III
Infantry Regiment
II
Three Infantry Battalions
III
Infantry Regiment
II
Three Infantry Battalions
X
Field Artillery Brigade
II
Cavalry Regiment
I
Four squadrons
III
Field Artillery Regiment
II
Art. Battalions
III
Field Artillery Regiment
II
Art. Battalions

German trucks lined up along the banks of the Daugava River in Riga, Russian Empire, in 1917. In the background are the iron railway bridges, with the old one, built in 1872, destroyed by shellfire and the new one inaugurated in 1914. (AC)

Motorcycles

An NSU motorcycle, the most likely model introduced in 1917 with the simplified torpedo-shaped fuel tank. The photograph is dated mid-1917 and made in *Kraftfahrerkaserne Lankwitz* (Motor Transport Troop Barracks near/in Berlin). (Photo: Arbeitskreis Historisches Lankwitz). The MK prefix in the registration number signifies that this vehicle was used on the home territory. Note that both soldiers wear leather biker uniforms and goggles. (AC)

A Wanderer motorcycle used by a messenger of the *VIII.Armee*. (AC)

Photograph featuring unidentified motorcycle units during a lull in combat. (AC)

In the autumn of 1915, Fresh Meat Motorized Columns were introduced with the reserve corps (the army corps already had these from September 1914) to better feed troops.

The Rear-Echelon Mot. Ambulance Det. (*Etappen-Sanitäts-Kraftwagen-Abteilungen*) were formed by concentrating ambulances from the previous army level.

The Motorcycle Detachments (*Kraftradfahrer-Abteilungen*) were put under the sole control of the *Etappert-Inspekteure*, the mail transport depots (*Post-Kraftwagen-Parks*) were equipped with eight vehicles each.

In the autumn of 1915, the Fresh Meat Motorized Columns were disbanded again. Instead, a Corps-level MV Transport Column (*Korps-Kraftwagen-Kolonne*) was established to now handle all types of supplies. All independent divisions received a *Divisions-Kraftwagen-Kolonne,* and each *Etappen-Inspektion* received (in addition to the *Etappen-Kraftwagen-Kolonne)* an additional *Etappen-Kraftwagen-Staffel* (squadron) with three columns each. Around the same time, the General Gouverment of occupied Warsaw (*General-Gouvernemcnt Warschau*) was reorganised after the *General-Gouvernement Belgien* role model.

Towards the end of 1915, ten of the heaviest artillery batteries were motorized, and in 1916, a *Fussartillerie-Park* was established for each *Armee.* These Parks catered to the *Fussartillerie Battalions,* consisting of nine trucks each. Additionally, each *Armee* received a *Fussartillerie-Munitions-Kolonne* to transport ammunition for the heavy batteries.

By the first anniversary of the war's outbreak, each Field Army boasted approximately 8,500 staff cars, 10,400 truck and lorries, and 1,700 thousand motorcycles.

In December **1916**, the Motorized Troops underwent a significant transformation, assigning part of their motor pool to the Air Service, now established as an independent branch of service. They were placed under the supervision of the Inspectorate of Mechanical Transport Services, operating under the overall authority of the Inspector General of Military Communications. However, operational control of this service in the field armies (including direct responsibility for the mechanical transport park) as well as within Germany itself, was exerted by the Chief of Mechanical Transport (*Chef des Feldkraftfahrwesens*), who was in turn directly responsible to the Quartermaster General in the General Staff.

In 1916, a decision was made to enhance the effectiveness of transport troops by centralizing them under the command of the *Armee Oberkommandoes / AOK.*

Motorized Field Post

During the Great War, the Feld Post system was established separately by the Prussian, Bavarian and Württemberg armies to handle mail for troops at the front. Each field post station was assigned a random number to keep the location and movements of individual unit's secret and to facilitate the sorting of the large volume of mail. The numbers included the necessary address information to ensure prompt and accurate delivery of letters, postcards, and parcels to the front lines. In the 1914-1916 period, military postal units, which employed hundreds of trucks, transported about 12 billion items (of which 7 billion arrived from the country to the front and 5 billion from the front to the rear).

The arrival of the Prussian mail truck (*Kaiserliche Deutsch. Feldpost, S 428 – Südarmee*) at a German field post office in the village of Filipowo, nowadays north-east Poland. (IWM)

Throughout 1916, the *Kraftfahrtruppen* experienced a notable shift from front rear areas (*Etappen*) to frontline formations (*Armee*), with a predominant deployment near combat zones.

A decree issued on 15 December 1916, mandated the reorganization of motor transport units, specifically targeting the conversion of the *Etappen KK's*, *Jäger* and *Kavallerie KK's*, as well as the *Fussartillerie-Munitions KK's*, placing them directly under the command of the motorized transport troops' commanding officer (*Kommandeur der Kraftwagentruppen*).

The 58 *Korps-Kraftwagen-Kolonnen* were reorganised into *Division-Kraftwagen-Kolonnen* in December 1916, each consisting of six to twelve lorries, a concept previously exclusive to independent divisions. These divisional motor transport columns gradually became standard in all of the army's active, reserve (*Ersatz*), and *Landwehr* divisions.

A *Kaiserlich Deutsche Feldpost* truck was captured in an unidentified Polish city on the Eastern Front. (AC)

A truck of the Bavarian *Feldpost* marked with the royal coat of arms. (AC)

Motorized Field Post

During the war, Germany occupied all or parts of 16 different countries (Western and Eastern Europe, Balkans, Middle East, and East Africa), with occupation mail organized in all of them. The quantity of military mail produced during this area was vast, considering that Germany had over 11 million men under arms for more than four years. However, *Feldpost* cards and letters back to Germany were free of postage for the soldiers, items mailed to other destinations required payment.

A *Kaiserlich Deutsche Felpost* truck navigating across a river in Galicia, in present-day Southern Poland or Ukraine. (AC)

A light *Kaiserlich Deutsche Feldpost* truck on the Western Front. The vehicle bears the individual number '62' and displays service markings indicating affiliation with *JKHD 14*. (AC)

A Bavarian field post service truck can be recognized by the royal coat of arms adorning it. The vehicle likely deviates from standard military colors, possibly appearing in a light grey. (AC)

That measure increased the number of *Divisons-Kraftwagen-Kolonnen* to a total of 236 (numbered 530-800).

On 15 December 1916, the Army High Command (*OHL*) promoted the Chief of Motor Vehicle Operations at the Supreme Headquarters (*Feldkraftahrchef im Grossen Hauptquartier*) to the rank of *Brigadekommandeur* and put him in charge of Commander-in-Chief of the Motor Transport Service in the field and in the homeland (*Oberste Leitung des Kraftfahrwesens im Veld und in der Heimat*). This new role subordinated to him the *Inspektion der Kraftfahrtruppen* in the Fatherland and put him in overall control.

All the 1916 measures created a better-functioning military transport service, yet the lack of available vehicles made it impossible to create a vehicle reserve even by early 1917.

Further regulations ensued on 19 March 1917, which stipulated the conversion of various motor transport columns into Army Motorized Transport Columns (*Armee-Kraftwagen-Kolonnen*) of equal strength and composition. Those lacking trucks with a total payload of 54 tons were instructed to make appropriate conversions.

Army Motorized Transport Columns (*Armee-Kraftwagen Kolonnen*) Nos. 1 - 200 were furnished with trucks with a load capacity of 4 tons, while columns Nos. 201-400 were equipped with trucks with a load capacity of 3 tons, yet both types maintained the same total payload of 54 tons. Nonetheless, the majority of rear area motor transport columns and some cavalry motor transport columns (*Etappen KK's + Kavallerie KK's*) already possessed a loading capacity of 54 tons.

Composition of Army Motorized Transport Columns (Armee Kraftwagen Kolonnen) after March 1917:

Nos. 1-200: 1 personnel car, two small trucks, 17 lorries, including one fuel truck, one mobile workshop, one equipment truck, and one trailer field kitchen; Total staff: 2 officers, 58 non-commissioned officers, ranks, and enlisted personnel.

Nos. 201-400: one personnel car, two small trucks, 22 lorries, two fuel trucks, one mobile workshop, one equipment truck, and one trailer field kitchen; total staff: 2 officers, 69 non-commissioned officers, ranks, and enlisted personnel.

A corresponding decree for the Bavarian contingent was issued on 30 March 1917. This decree mandated the immediate conversion of all Bavarian Rear Echelon Motorized Transport Columns, Cavalry Motorized Transport Columns, Rear Echelon Ammunition Motorized Transport Columns, and Foot Artillery Ammunition Motorized Transport Columns into Bavarian Army Motorized Transport Columns. The Bavarian Army Motorized Transport Columns (*Armee-Kraftwagen-Kolonnen*) Nos. 171 - 186 were to be equipped with trucks with a load capacity of 4 tons, while columns Nos. 271 - 280 and Nos. 370 - 378 were to be outfitted with trucks with a load capacity of 3 tons.

By June 1917, all independent Transport Squadrons (*Kraftwagen-Staffeln*) underwent a name change to *Armee-Kraftwagen-Staffeln* and issued sequential numbers, though they kept their tasks such as training, replacement vehicle supply, fuel supply and so forth. Each *Armee-Kraftwagen-Staffel* was subdivided into three sections, each with the following equipment: 10 light trucks, 10 medium trucks, 30 heavy trucks and 6-10 motorized harvester ploughs in *Kraftpflug-Abteilungen*.

At around the same time, the field post transport columns (*Postkraftwagen-Parks*) were integrated into the *Armee-Kraftwagen-Staffeln*.

Wartime trucks and lorries
German columns on the advance to Nestle. The great German offensive in the West, April 1918. (Photo: National Archives and Record Administration / NARA)

Motorized Transport Troops responsible for supply transport, in full-leather uniform (cap, jacket, trousers, boots) in front of a 3-ton lorry. Note the *JKD 7* temporary markings of the *Immobiles Kraftwagen Depot* (Stationary Motor Vehicles Depot) painted on the load box. (AC)

A light truck of the 53rd Field Flight Detachment (*Feld-Flieg-Abt-53*). (AC)

Wartime trucks and lorries.
In the later stages of the war, transporting wounded soldiers to hospitals beyond the war zone relied heavily on a wide range of trucks, buses, and staff cars, as the availability of motorized ambulances was severely restricted. (AC)

French prisoners of war aboard a German heavy lorry. This is an unique sight, as POWs rarely had access to the luxury of motorized transportation. (AC)

A Dux truck assigned to the *XIX.(Home) Armee* is recognizable due to its registration number with MK prefix (MK XIX 393). (AC)

The 23 *Kommandeure der Kraftfahrtruppen* at various *Etappen-Inspektionen* were reassigned to the *AOK.'s* as *Kommandeure der Kraftfahrtruppen* under their respective *AOK's*.

The Rear-Echelon Parks / Depots (*Etappen-Kraftwagen-Parks*) underwent a name change to *Armee-Kraftwagen-Parks* and were centrally numbered. Their responsibilities included supplying personnel, vehicles, parts, and fuel for the squadrons (*Staffeln*) and performing vehicle maintenance. Additionally, they provided both fixed and mobile fuel stations.

The Rear Area Motorized Medical Detachments (*Etappen-Sanka*) were also removed from *Etappen* command and transformed into *Sanitäts-Kraftwagen-Abteilungen* at the *Armee* level, as well as the Heavy Artillery Vehicle Parks (*Fussartillerie-Kraftzug-Parks*), which evolved into artillery tractor parks (*Armee-Fussartillerie-Kraftzug-Parks*) and were increased from seven to ten such units.

In **1917**, the reserve of the Land Forces (*Heeres-Reserve*) was established, aiming to utilize it as a rapid deployment force. To facilitate their movement to critical points on the front, the still-existing 9 *Jaeger KK*, 52 *Kavallerie KK's*, 102 *Etappen KK's, and* 33 *Fussartillerie Munition KK's* were reformed into *Armee KK's*.

In May 1917, field armies could also rely on twenty Motorcycle Detachments (*Kraftradfahrer-Abteilungen*), numbered 1 to 20, eleven fortress car parks, eight auxiliary vehicles detachments, one motorcycle depot, ten stationary car depots, and fifteen Stationary Motor Vehicles Depots (*Immobile-Kraftwagen-Depots / JKD*) namely: *JKD 1* Düsseldorf, *JKD 2* Cöln Deuz, *JKD 3/4* Frankfurt a./ Main, *JKD 5* Mannheim, *JKD 7* Untertürkheim, *JKD. 8* Berlin Schöneberg, *JKD 9* Breslau, *JKD 10* Stettin, *JKD 11* Zwikau, *JKHD 1* Bremen, *JKHD 3* Braunschweig, *JKHD 12* Elbing, *JKD* Nürberg.

Introduced in 1917, and expanded in 1918, new tactical approach based on specially trained assault troops (*Sturmtruppen*) made it necessary to boost transport capacities. To cope with such a challange, the Army High Command (*OHL*) converted the following additional units to *Armee-Kraftwagen-Kolonnen* for ammunition (*munitions*) transport under direct army-level command:

Jäger-Munitions-Kraftwagen-Kolonnen (9 columns)
Kavallerie-Munitions-Kraftwagen-Kolonnen (52 columns)
Etappen-Munitions-Kraftwagen-Kolonnen (102 columns)
Fussartillerie-Munitions-Kraftwagen-Kolonnen (32 columns)

The Army Transport Troops were reorganized into a total of *zur besonderen Verfügung* (special army transport columns), with the numbering ranging from 1 to 384 (not all numbers used sequentially). Field Armies were assigned 234 transport columns (*Armee KK's*); numbers 1-130 and 171-384), divisions - 215 columns *(Divisions KK's)*; numbers 530-800). Some independent companies also received their columns (26 columns with numbers 1-23, 30, 51-52).

The Emperor and his cars
During the Great War, Kaiser (Emperor) Wilhelm II, as a forward-thinking monarch, embraced the use of automobiles to demonstrate technological advancement and efficiency.
Kaiser Wilhelm II and Kronprinzen (Crown Prince) during a field inspection in 1915. (AC)

Besides wheeled transport vehicles, a few tracked supply carrier columns (*Raupen-Kolonnen*) were formed to transport ammunition over rough terrain. Numbered 1111-1115 and 1117, they were equipped with the *A7V Überland-Geländewagen* (56 pieces), constructed on the same chassis as the *A7V* tank. The armor was replaced by two cargo platforms, front and rear, designed to navigate shell craters in roads and terrain, making ammunition transport more manageable. Transport column 1116 was equipped with *Orionwagen* vehicles, using the pedrail system instead of tracks.

Kaiser Wilhelm II arriving by car at Udine on the Italian Front, November 1917. Udine was taken by the Austro-Hungarian and German Armies on 29 October 1917. (AC)

A *Stab* car (Mercedes) dedicated to transporting high-rank officers. The closed (or semi-closed) cabs ensured that the officers could maintain communication and operational planning while on the move, making it a practical choice for high-level military transportation. (AC)

Military vehicle markings
A staff car (NAG) from the Prussian army detachment can be identified due to the black Reichadler symbol. Note the *JKD 8* service marking of the *Immobile-Kraftwagen-Park* in Berlin. (AC)

Bavarian supply troops pose in fatigued uniforms with kitchen equipment and beer mugs. Note the crowned blue-and-white Bavarian coat of arms on the vehicle side. (AC)

A staff car (*Stabwagen*) marked with the minor Würtemburg coat of arms. (AC)

In April **1918**, two *Feldrekrufendepots der Kraftfahrtruppen* were created to recruit new personnel for the motor transport forces.

Also in 1918 arose the problem of equipping artillery units (hitherto horse-drawn) with motor vehicles. In a maximum effort based on the weak resources available that late in the war, one motorized transport squadron (*Kraftwagen-Staffel*) was issued to each of the six field artillery regiments (*Feldartillerie-Regimenter*) and five heavy artillery battalions (*Fussartillerie-Bataillone*).

2.3 Daily service

The responsibility for managing these supply columns fell to the column leader (*Kolonnen-Führer*). This role was critical, as the leader was tasked with ensuring that the load was properly managed, including strict adherence to maximum load limits and careful weight distribution on the cargo decks of the trucks. Improper loading could lead to mechanical failures or accidents, especially in the demanding conditions often faced by military supply convoys. Before embarking on a mission, it was the *Kolonnen-Führer*'s duty to ensure that the column was adequately provisioned with necessary food supplies for the crews. This was essential, as the crews needed to be sustained throughout potentially long and arduous journeys. All details regarding the loads, including the specific types of equipment and supplies being transported, had to be meticulously documented in official records. This documentation was vital not only for logistical tracking but also for accountability; any losses that occurred in transit had to be reported immediately, ensuring that there was a clear record of any discrepancies between the dispatched and received goods.

When it came to the transport of ammunition, additional precautions were required due to the inherent dangers involved. Ammunition loads were ideally transferred directly from railroad supply trains at railroad stations to the trucks, which would then transport these critical supplies to field ammunition depots. This direct transfer minimized handling and reduced the risk of accidents or delays. However, during combat situations, the columns might be ordered to deliver ammunition directly to frontline units, specifically to their artillery positions. This task was especially perilous, as it often involved navigating through areas under enemy fire.

Given the volatility of the cargo, the loading of ammunition was always supervised by an officer to ensure that all safety protocols were strictly followed. In addition, explosive ordnance personnel were assigned to the truck columns. These specialists were responsible for repacking or handling the ammunition if any adjustments were needed during the journey, beyond the initial loading and unloading. Their presence was crucial in preventing accidents that could result from improper handling or the need to make changes to the load configuration *en route*.

When the trucks formed a marching column, strict discipline was maintained in terms of spacing between vehicles. This distance was determined by a combination of factors, including road conditions, the speed of the convoy, and the braking capabilities of the trucks. Under routine conditions—dry weather and hard roads—the standard distance between vehicles was typically 10-12 meters. This spacing was sufficient to allow dispatch riders, usually on motorcycles, to pass between the trucks as they carried orders and communications up and down the column.

Military drivers

With the outbreak of the Great War, there was an immediate need for military drivers. Those interested had to undergo training at driving schools (*Fahrschulen*). The training was rudimentary, particularly given that many recruits, including even chauffeurs accustomed to passenger cars, lacked experience in driving heavy trucks. Prospective drivers often only needed to demonstrate basic engine control and vehicle maneuvering within the confines of military depot yards to acquire their licenses.

A staff car (*Phänomen 14 35 PS Tourenwagen*) from the *Kraftfahr Batl. Fahrschulen*. The license plate with the prefix (MK) was used on the homeland territory after 1 December 1914. (AC)

A *Fahrschule* truck of the *VII Armee* from the training facilities situated deep within the Imperial Territory (the Grand Duchy of Hesse?) This photo was taken in mid-1915. (AC)

A staff car from the 11th Vehicles Reserve Detachment, Driving School (*Kraft. Ers. Abt. 11 / Fahrschule*). (AC)

Rear-Echelon / Sector Military Depot
The Etappen-Kraftwagen-Park Armee Abt. Strantz used technical facilities taken from the French machinery factory of M. Theobald. The photo shows vehicles with tactical markings identing vehicles of the 94.I.D. = *94. Inf.Div.*, V. A.K. = *V. Armeekorps.* (AC)

The *Etappen-Kraftwagen-Park* based in Metz in 1918. A noteworthy staff car bearing a civilian registration number (marked with the IIID prefix, indicating a district in Württemberg) and displaying a white *Reichsadler* as a sign identifying a military vehicle. Could this have been a recently confiscated car? (AC)

The *Etappen-Kraftwagen-Park Armee Abt. Strantz* was located in Metz Nord, on the route to Thionville, France 1918. (AC)

In more challenging conditions, such as hilly terrain or steep climbs, each truck might need to tackle obstacles individually. In these situations, the column would temporarily disperse, with each vehicle crossing the obstacle on its own before regrouping on the other side. This method ensured that each truck could navigate the difficult terrain without being impeded by the vehicle in front of it. Other factors that could necessitate larger gaps between vehicles included the presence of dust, which could obscure visibility, or ice, which would reduce traction and increase stopping distances. If the spacing between trucks became too great—potentially risking a breakdown in communication or coordination—the leading vehicles were required to slow down until the entire column was back in formation. This careful management of spacing was crucial for maintaining the integrity and efficiency of the convoy, ensuring that supplies reached their destination in a timely manner.

The last vehicle in the column was typically a bus (*Kraftomnibus*), which served multiple roles. It often carried additional personnel, provided rear security, and acted as a signal to the column leader that all vehicles were still in place. This vehicle was also useful for picking up any soldiers who might have been left behind or for dealing with emergencies at the rear of the column.

The *Kraftfahrtruppe* officers in operational reports indicated that driving and truck management was an exceptionally stressful role for drivers; thus, to help reduce the burden German trucks usually had three drivers (assistant drivers) assigned to them, but maintaining such a high number of personnel was not always possible.

After a typical ten-hour workday, the crew assigned to operate and maintain cargo trucks faced a grueling routine that extended well beyond their formal shifts. Following their workday, these individuals were required to engage in a rigorous regimen of maintenance and minor repairs on their vehicles. This essential upkeep was necessary to ensure that the vehicles remained operational and reliable under the harsh conditions of the front lines. The nature of their work meant that they often had to address mechanical issues, perform routine checks, and make small adjustments or fixes to keep the vehicles in good working order.

Once the maintenance tasks were completed, the crew's day was far from over. They had to settle for a meager meal, which typically provided insufficient nourishment to sustain them through the demanding physical and mental strains of their duties. The conditions in which they lived were equally harsh, as they were forced to endure lice-infested field quarters. These living conditions not only contributed to discomfort but also posed significant health risks, exacerbating the challenges faced by the crew.

In the winter months, the difficulties of their situation were compounded by the severe weather. The cold temperatures increased the risk of illnesses such as pneumonia and hypothermia. The inadequate heating in their field quarters and the exposure to the elements during their work further heightened these risks. Crew members had to deal with frostbite, hypothermia, and other cold-related health issues while continuing their demanding work schedules

Interestingly, in March 1918, 50,000 trained drivers and mechanics were transferred away from the *Kraftfahruppen* into the infantry, with their roles being filled by very young and inexperienced recruits who received just a few weeks of training. Although the German Army was desperate for front-line soldiers this move immediately backfired with large numbers of mechanical failures and within the *VII.Armee* alone 1,400 accidents were attributed to this reorganisation.

Rear-Echelon/Sector Military Depot
A motor depot of the *III.Armee* which operated throughout the entire Great War on the Western Front, initially in Belgium but primarily in France. This particular transport column was fortunate to be based under a roof, utilizing a factory depot taken from its French owners. (AC)

Field forges (*Feldschmieden*) were specifically utilized for tasks related to the chassis and suspensions of various military equipment. Skilled mechanics used them to carry out on-the-spot repairs, reinforcing or reshaping metal components, and addressing any structural issues that arose. (AC)

Motorized support troops were responsible for tasks such as recovering damaged vehicles. In the photo, recovery soldiers from the *VI. Armee* transport column (Arras, France, December 1917) are salvaging one of their valuable trucks. The towing vehicle is another standard cargo truck, in this case a NAG, as the German Army had very few designated wreckers at that time. (AC)

Rear-Echelon/Sector Military Depot
A field depot stocked with rubber tires suggests that the photo was taken at the beginning of the war. Over time, the extensive blockade imposed by the Allies led to severe shortages of raw materials in Germany, including rubber. This forced the Imperial Army to experiment with full-metal spring wheels. (AC)

A commemorative photo of a group of automotive or aircraft mechanics, proving that repairs of simple internal combustion engines could be conducted in field conditions. (AC)

Motor depots in territories occupied by the Germans were preferably located in large mechanical facilities that, before the war, produced agricultural machinery, railway rolling stock or motor vehicles. In the field, blacksmith workshops were adopted for the repair of severely damaged vehicles. (AC)

2.4 Support services

The Stationary Motor Vehicles Depots (*JKD's*) were tasked with the temporary storage, transportation, and deployment of military vehicles between factories and the battlefield. Thirteen units were established across the homeland, responsible for the entire process, from coordinating with factories to deploying assets to the required locations or field units.

The field maintenance model provided by Motor Vehicles Parks (*Kraftwagen-Parken*), was marked by a combination of basic maintenance practices, field repair workshops, and the need for improvisation due to supply chain challenges.

Motor Parks were strategically positioned behind the front lines. These units, often located on factory premises, provided shelter for mobile facilities concealed beneath large tent canvases. The setup included various workshops such as a smithy for axle repairs, a carpentry shop for bodywork, a glassworks, a plumber's shop, a saddlery, a tailor shop, and even a shoemaker's shop. An engine overhaul column addressed worn-out motors, frequently requiring new bearings. A rubber depot patched covers and inner tubes, while a generator truck supplied artificial light for the facility and power for the electric motors in the repair shop. When the *Feldschmiede* (field forge) was set up, special fire prevention measures had to be implemented.

A *Kraftwagen-Park* also ensured the Army›s fuel, oil, tires, spare parts, and tools supply.
Defective or damaged vehicles were gathered for salvage, with usable parts extracted. The remaining vehicles were stored at a 'graveyard' near the motor park until rail transport to factories could be arranged. Consequently, the park staff maintained an extensive storehouse of raw materials, including spring steel, iron, and brass, for its own use and for the mobile repair shops. These mobile facilities, dedicated to smaller repairs, closely followed motorized troop units to address issues promptly on-site.

Less complicated truck repairs were expected to be undertaken by the drivers themselves in the field. To assist them, each motor transport column of 25 trucks was equipped with a workshop truck, which, with their machine tools, would help repair or make new parts as and when necessary to keep the other trucks on the road.

Stationary Fuel Stations (*Immobile Tankstellen*) were assigned to all *JKD* units. In addition, each corps and independent division was equipped with its own Mobile Fuel Station (*Bewegliche Tankstelle*). These stations were designed to move with the unit, providing a continuous supply of fuel as the frontlines shifted. This was particularly important for maintaining the momentum of offensives and ensuring that vehicles, from trucks to tanks, could operate without interruption.

Cavalry divisions, which were typically more mobile and less equipped with motor vehicles, relied on the nearest corps or divisions for their fuel needs, integrating into the broader logistical network rather than maintaining independent fuel stations.

The operational procedure for mobile fuel stations was structured to maintain readiness and efficiency. After distributing fuel, these stations were required to return to an *Etappen-Kraftwagen-Park* or another major storage location to replenish their supplies. However, to ensure continuous support, at least one mobile fuel station had to remain operational within the unit at all times, ready to meet immediate fuel demands.

Rear-Echelon/Sector Military Depot
Photo take in the *Bayrische-Etappen-Kraftwagen-Park 6* from the *VI.Armee*. One of the mechanics paints a white background on a truck bonnet for tactical markings. (AC)

The *Kraftwagen-Park 505* based in Tiberiade, Palestine in 1917-18. (AC)

German *Kraftwagen-Park* somewhere in the Balkans. Note soldiers with fuel drums most likely serving with an *Immobile Tanksletten* (stationary fuel station) which were attached to all immobile motor depots. (AC)

Staff cars

When the war broke out, the Imperial Army had only a limited number of staff cars. They were mostly acquired via the Imperial Volunteer Automobile Corps or confiscated from civilians. Staff cars were generally reserved for officers, except for vehicles converted with the help of special bodies to various types of special-purpose vehicles.

A staff car (*Bergmann Metallurgique*) which was photographed in 1914. Note the civil registration number (II-5500) of the District Authority Dresden and the Saxon coat of arms painted on the side doors, the driver wears the black leather uniform of the *Kraftfahrtruppen.* (AC)

Horch 8/24 PS, reg. number IIM-785, with Bavarian Coat of Arms. (AC)

A staff car used by the CO of the *Festung* (Fortress) Strasburg marked with the Imperial eagle symbol. (AC)

A typical *Bewegliche Tankstelle* consisted of one truck manned by a junior non-commissioned officer (NCO). The truck was stocked with a comprehensive inventory to meet the immediate needs of the unit: 3 tons of petrol stored in oil drums, 200 kg of oil, 20 kg of grease, 100 kg of carbide (used for lighting), 20 kg of cotton waste for cleaning, 30 kg of petroleum, and 250 kg of rubber spare parts. This supply was calculated to sustain an army corps for up to three days under peacetime conditions. However, during the intense and prolonged operations of later war years, the demand for these supplies, particularly fuel, increased significantly, straining the logistical system.

To facilitate the operation of these mobile fuel stations, they were equipped with essential tools and equipment, including fuel pumps for efficient refueling, buckets and funnels for handling fuel, and lamps for nighttime operations. This equipment ensured that the stations could function around the clock, crucial during continuous operations.

All *Tankstellen* (both immobile and mobile) were marked for easy identification. Each was equipped with a sign or flag bearing the words *Betriebsstoffe für Kraftfahrzeuge* (Operating Supplies for Motor Vehicles) in black lettering on a yellow background. This signage ensured that every motor vehicle within the army could easily locate and access the fuel stations.

2.5 Wartime vehicles production

In 1918, the number of German military transport vehicles reached approximately 40,200 (including 12,000 staff cars, 25,000 truck and lorries, plus motorcycles and artillery tractors) out of a total of 69,977 officially delivered to the army (plus impressed vehicles). The number was significant considering the starting level of 1914 but much lower than the 200,000 motor vehicles that the Allies (Entente) had at their disposal at the war's end. Mass production was achieved due to standardization, which hardly existed in the German motor vehicle industry before 1914. Only when the war broke out did the Automotive Testing Commission (*ATK*) initiate the process of advanced standardization of motor vehicle components, such as the part for igniters, carburetors, brake systems, etc., as well as the entire truck's design. The standardization process also covered tire sizes. It was an enormous effort, as instead of 120 different dimensions for pneumatic tires and 170 for solid rubber tires, nine standard sizes were now defined.

Truck and lorries delivered to the Imperial Army between 1914-1918 (estimated number excluding minority producers)

Type / Payload	Pieces	Manufacturers	
Truck / 5 tons	816	*Hansa-Lloyd*	10,600
Truck / 4t	11,030	*Benz*	6,150
Truck / 3t	22,230	*Daimler-Marienfelde*	3,680
Truck / 2t	2,764	*Horch*	1,790
Truck / 1 or 1,5 t	1,274	*Stoewer*	1,760
Trailers	6,494	*Deutz*	1,350
Ambulances	4,004	*Vomag*	1,000
Military Postal Service	156	*MAN*	990
Special purpose vehicles	1,434	*Adler*	900
Total	**50,202**		

Super-heavy lorries
The *Krupp-Daimler K.D.I Artillerieschlepper* was equipped with a 100hp (delivering peak power at 1200 rpm) four-cylinder engine with a working volume of 12 litres. By itself, the lorry weighed 7.4 tons and could tow a trailer weighing 15 tons. The maximum speed did not exceed 35km/h, and the gasoline consumption was 100 litres per 100km on a flat road and 150 litres per 100km on rough terrain. (AC)
A late-war variant of *K.D. I* from the *IV.Armee.* The rear view reveals the massive cargo bay designed for carrying heavy artillery ammunition, while the side benches were occupied by a gun crew of 8-10 soldiers. (AC)

A *K.D.I* lorry painted with *Feldgrau* (field grey). It has the temporary markings of the J.K.D.7 located below the cabin door. (AC)

A *K.D. I* from. unknown unit, 1917. Note that the soldiers wear puttees and boots, not the pre-war marching jackboots typical for infantry. The dress code is usual for the rear-army sector motor depot. (AC)

The Büssing K.W.Z. 1800 heavy artillery tractor was used to tow the Krupp 21cm Mörser, deployed by Heavy Artillery Regiments (*Fussartillerie Rgt)*, most of which served on the Western Front from 1914 to 1918. From 1 December 1914—following an ordinance issued on 27 November—the black *Reichsadler* on a white shield (Prussian coat of arms) was adopted as the marking for all non-combat motor vehicles, including artillery tractors, belonging to Prussian formations. Initially, the eagle emblem was applied only to vehicles allocated to front-line units. (Artwork by David Bocquelet)

A Daimler-Marienfelde truck from an unidentified Prussian Motor Vehicle Column (*Preussische Kraftwagen-Kolonne*) on the Western Front, 1917. The vehicle is finished in the standard *Feldgrau* (field-grey) paint of the period, with wheels, chassis, and metal fittings typically painted in the same tone for uniformity and reduced visibility. Canvas tilt and side panels were likely khaki or grey-brown, weathered by heavy use. Such trucks were used for transporting ammunition, rations, and engineering stores, and were often seen caked in mud from the shell-torn supply routes leading toward the front. (Artwork by David Bocquelet)

Late-war (1918) Krupp-Daimler K.D.I heavy lorry, used both as a heavy artillery tractor and as an ammunition transporter near the front lines. While not usually exposed to direct enemy fire, these vehicles were camouflaged to reduce the risk of aerial attack. This example is painted in a disruptive pattern of *Feldgrau* (green-grey), *Ocker* (ochre), *Braun* (brown), and *Rotbraun* (red-brown), separated by 5 cm Schwarz (black) lines.

Introduced late in the war, the Krupp-Daimler K.D.I provided essential mobility in difficult and often treacherous terrain where other vehicles struggled to operate effectively. Its powerful engine and rugged construction enabled it to transport heavy loads of large-caliber ammunition, artillery pieces, and other critical supplies, ensuring sustained firepower and reliable logistical support close to the front lines. Its ability to handle demanding terrain and heavy cargo significantly enhanced the operational flexibility of German artillery units in 1918 and contributed to the development of post-war German armored military vehicles. (Artwork by David Bocquelet)

Krupp 21 cm Mörser in towed position, painted in a patchy camouflage scheme typical of late-war German heavy artillery to help conceal the massive siege mortar from enemy observation and aerial reconnaissance. Due to its weight, the Mörser had to be broken down into several parts (barrel, carriage, etc.) for long-distance transport. However, on the battlefield, if the terrain allowed and for short-range movement, it could be towed as a whole. (Artwork by David Bocquelet)

An early Podeus LIII heavy lorry, produced for the Imperial Army under the Ministry of War's subsidy program, was delivered to the 1st Company of the 1st Motor Transport Battalion (*Kraftfahr-Bataillon*) shortly before the outbreak of the First World War. During 1914–1915, these vehicles transported supplies to positions at least 10 kilometers from the front lines, making the use of disruptive camouflage unnecessary. (Artwork by David Bocquelet)

Mercedes of the Imperial Volunteer Automobile Corps (*Kaiserlichen-Freiwilligen-Automobil-Corps*), operating within Imperial territory, were authorized to carry registration plates with numbers painted in red. A special sign was affixed beside the rear plate: a red square (12 × 12cm) with a yellow square at its center, bearing the letters 'K.F.A.C.' in each corner. Vehicles serving in rear sectors of the front were painted green-grey (*Feldgrau*) and marked with two broad crimson stripes on the body and bonnet. In 1916, the corps was renamed the Imperial Automobile Corps (*K.Kf.K., Kaiserliches Kraftfahr-Korps*), a change that may have affected its markings, though details remain unknown. (Artwork by David Bocquelet)

Staff car of Admiral Ludwig von Schröder, *Marinekorps Flandern*, 1917, bearing the unit emblem of two crossed anchors topped with a crown and flanked by flowing sashes. Originally embroidered on naval infantry shoulder straps since the early 20th century, the symbol became widely used after the outbreak of war. Painted on a white shield, it appeared on both sides of staff cars and on lories used by naval infantry. This vehicle also carried the Imperial German Admiral's pennant. (Artwork by David Bocquelet)

Opel 3-ton truck from an unidentified Bavarian Motor Vehicle Column (*Bayerische Kraftwagen-Kolonne*) serving with the *V. Armee* on the Western Front in 1918. It bears the lesser Bavarian coat of arms—a crowned escutcheon of white and blue oblique fusils—along with unidentified unit tactical symbols resembling a flower. (Artwork by David Bocquelet)

Staff cars
Staff cars used during the Great War were typically modified civilian automobiles, capable of carrying 4 to 6 passengers. (AC)

A staff car (Opel 35?) from the 41st Air Service Detachment (*HQ Feld Luftschiff Abt 41*). Photo taken in December 1917 on the Western Front. (AC)

A postcard photo taken outside the Grand Hotel Britannique in Belgium, which served as an HQ for the German Army during the First World War. (AC)

While precise production statistics for passenger cars during the war years are challenging to determine, it is clear that the output of civilian vehicles declined sharply. The war effort consumed vast amounts of resources including skilled labor which was redirected towards the production of military vehicles and other war-related industries. Despite the decline in production, the number of cars available to the German Army by the end of the war exceeded 10,000. This was primarily due to the requisitioning of civilian cars that had been produced before the outbreak of the war. The German military also benefited from private donations, particularly from members of the Imperial Automobile Club and the German Automobile Corps (*Kaiserliches Automobil-Korps*).

The method of acquiring vehicles—through requisition and private donations—resulted in an enormous mix of types and models within the military's vehicle fleet. This diversity posed challenges in terms of maintenance and repair, as the wide range of vehicles required different parts and expertise. However, it also meant that the German Army had access to a broad array of vehicles, which could be adapted for various purposes (e.g. ambulances or radio mast carriers).

Despite the challenges, several key manufacturers played a significant role in supplying vehicles to the military. These included Adler, Benz, Daimler and Opel.

Passenger cars production statistics

Selected manufacturers	Production period	Pieces (est.)	Selected models by engine type
Benz	1885-1918	18,000	16/40hp (1915-20), 33/70hp (1912-1916), 16/40hp (1913-20)
Opel	1899-1918	18,000	5/14hp, 40/100hp
Daimler (Mercedes)	1890-1918	13,590	8/22 (1913-21), 12-32 (1915-19), 22/50hp (1912-12), 28/60hp (1910-20)
Adler	1899-1918	14,000	30/70hp (1911-14), 35/80hp (1911-14), 25/55hp (1913-1914), 30/70hp (1911-14)
Protos	1901-1918	5,000-10,000	26/50hp (1908-14), 27/65hp (1908-14), 18/45hp (1910-12)
Hansa-Lloyd	1907-1918	5,000	22/50hp (1910-14)
Polyphon (Dux)	1904-1918	700	8/21hp (1910-13), 10/30hp (1912-14) 6/18hp (1912-19)
Presto	1908-1918	850	8/222hp (1910-12), 6/18hp (1913+), 8/25hp (1913+)

Although the manufacturers were restricted in their design freedom by these coercive measures, they received lucrative military orders in return. They belonged to the branches of industry that profited greatly from the war economy. The benefits went beyond road vehicle production as Daimler or Opel also manufactured aircraft engines similar to those in motor vehicles.

Standardization slowed during the second half of the Great War due to a permanent shortage of raw materials and a drop in material quality, which could not be remedied with substitutes. It also hardly touched the motorcycle and car sectors; however, the foundation of the Standards Committee of German Industry (*Der Normenausschusses der Deutschen Industr*ie) in 1917 at the latest paved the way for the more efficient production process in the post-war period.

Production range

While the German automotive industry struggled to produce a sufficient quantity of motor vehicles during the war, its product range was comparable to that of the Allies.

Motorcycles: Wanderer and NSU produced excellent motorcycles, which were used on all fronts. The example in the photo shows a motorcycle used by a messenger serving with *Armee-Abteilung D* in 1917-1918. (AC)

Staff Cars: Staff cars were primarily supplied by Benz, Daimler, and Opel. The photo presents an interesting example of a staff car with the tactical markings of the *VII. Armee* on the bonnet, service markings of *JKD ¾* based in Frankfurt a./Main on the driver's cabin door, and the national identification sign, the Imperial eagle. (AC)

Super-Heavy Lorries were produced by Krupp-Daimler. The vehicle in the photo could potentially be a *Ballon-Kraftzugmaschine* from the *IV. Armee*, featuring special winches mounted on top of the load box. In December 1917, the *Royal Bayerischen Inspektion des Militär-Luftfahrwesens* ordered twelve of these vehicles. (AC)

Staff cars

While trucks were primarily produced for transportation troops, staff cars had a broader allocation across various branches of the military, however most of them were reserved for use by high-ranking officers as their personal means of transportation. This distinction highlighted the staff car's role not just as a vehicle, but as a symbol of authority and command within the military hierarchy, ensuring that senior officers could move swiftly and efficiently across the theater of operations. The car in the photo, based on the registration prefix (MK), was used by a reserve unit of the home army. (AC)

A staff car used by the pilots of the *FAA 34* at Cunle airfield in the winter of 1914-15. (AC)

Officers from an unidentified Bavarian unit of the *VI.Armee* photographed on the Italian Front. (AC)

2.6 Shortages of strategic materials

As the First World War dragged on, the shortage of strategic materials became a pressing issue, particularly impacting the motor industry. The Allied naval blockade significantly exacerbated this problem, restricting Germany's ability to import crucial resources such as rubber and fuel oils.

At the start of the war, Germany's gasoline reserves were relatively substantial, standing at around 76,000 tons. However, these supplies were quickly depleted due to the high demands of both civilian and military vehicles. The situation worsened with the loss of access to essential resources from Galicia and Romania, which were key suppliers of raw materials. To address the fuel shortage, Germany began producing benzol, a coal-tar derivative that could be used as a substitute for gasoline.

By 1915, in response to the growing scarcity and the need to prioritize military needs, the Quartermaster General implemented stringent regulations. These guidelines restricted motor vehicle traffic within Germany to only essential services, ensuring that available fuel was allocated primarily to war-related activities. Additionally, the military requisitioned more motor vehicles for service in the war effort, further intensifying the consumption of available fuel supplies.

Despite these measures, the consumption of fuels, including those derived from benzol, surged. The military command took control of the distribution of fuels that could be mixed with benzol, attempting to maximize the efficiency of the limited fuel resources. Nevertheless, the allocation of fuel remained a contentious issue. A significant portion of the available fuel reserves was prioritized for the German Navy's submarines and the air service, leaving transport troops with insufficient supplies. This allocation reflected the strategic priority given to naval and aerial operations over ground transport.

The rubber shortage that emerged at the onset of the war further compounded the difficulties. Rubber was essential for manufacturing tires, but with limited supplies, Germany faced a severe shortage. By 1915, the scarcity of rubber led to the adoption of iron-shod wheels and steel tires on many motor vehicles. These alternatives, while functional, were less effective and more prone to wear compared to rubber tires, which affected the efficiency and operational capability of the motorized units.

2.7 Motorized transport troops at the war's end

On 11 November 1918, the Imperial German Army found itself in a dire situation regarding its remaining resources and equipment. Among the various assets still at its disposal were thousands of trucks. As part of the armistice agreements, these vehicles were to be handed over to the Allied forces.

The backbone of the supply chain
One of the most crucial roles that trucks played was in the transportation of foodstuffs. Keeping troops well-fed was a top priority, and the logistical demands of delivering fresh food to soldiers in the trenches were immense. Unlike horse-drawn carts, trucks could carry larger loads, travel longer distances, and navigate difficult terrain more effectively, making them indispensable in the complex supply networks of the time.
A truck from the Bavarian *EKK 4* carrying a large load of grain destined for delivery to a field bakery. (AC)

Despite the official orders to surrender these trucks, many German units, acting either out of defiance or in an attempt to deny resources to the Allies, decided to destroy their motor pools instead.

Some German operators, determined to return home with their vehicles, attempted to drive them back to Germany. However, the ravages of war had left the infrastructure in poor condition, and many of these trucks broke down along the way. Stranded in France or Belgium, these non-operational vehicles were left behind by their drivers.

The local civilian populations in these regions, recovering from the war and in need of resources, quickly absorbed the abandoned trucks. The trucks found new life in the hands of farmers, businesses, and other civilians, serving as a testament to the adaptability and resilience of the people in war-torn areas.

Trucks from the Bavarian *EKK 9*, assigned to the *IV.Armee*, ready for a food supply mission. (AC)

A long column of supply trucks, likely photographed in the Carpathian Mountains in 1916. (AC)

Trucks to remember
Soldiers of motorized units often posed in front of their trucks for photographs, capturing moments of camaraderie and pride. Motorized vehicles, being relatively new in military operations at the time, represented technological advancement and were a source of pride for those who operated them. Trucks from unidentified transport column from the *IV.Armee* in France. Note the French POW in dark coat standing in the center as an 'additional attraction'. (AC)

The action shots, though less common, provide a vivid contrast to the more posed and formal commemorative photos. Photo taken by soldiers of the *VII. Armee* in 1917. (AC)

Most commemorative photos from the Great War were static, reflecting the limitations of photography at the time and the desire to capture clear, composed images. (AC)

Shortages of strategic materials

Solid rubber tires were a practical choice for military trucks due to their durability and resistance to punctures, however by 1917-18 the rubber shortage led to the use of all metal tires.

An Adler truck from the *I.Armee* equipped with solid rubber tires taking a break during travel somewhere in France. (AC)

A German column moving through the town of Armentières, located in northern France near the Belgian border. The photo proves that trucks equipped with solid rubber tires could withstand the wear and tear of continuous use across various terrains, including muddy tracks. (AC)

Solid rubber tires were used by all German truck manufacturers, including the well-known Benz, which featured the popular *Kettenwagen Typ 3K2* model. (AC)

German transport troops in the Middle East
While most Imperial German motorized transport formations were deployed in Europe, some vehicles were also sent to the Middle East, where they faced unique logistical challenges posed by the harsh desert terrain, extreme temperatures, and vast distances between key locations.
A German military ambulance in Palestine, marked with the Red Cross, symbolized humanitarian efforts. Although the Ottoman Empire recognized the Red Cross, it established its own equivalent, the Red Crescent Society, to serve similar humanitarian purposes within the context of Islamic culture. (AC)

A group of German and Ottoman soldiers with their *Benz* trucks posing for the camera in Palestine, 1917-18. (AC)

A column of lorries is seen towing 15cm *schwere Feld Haubitze (s.F.H.)* 1913, while also transporting limbers in their load boxes. (AC)

3
Motor Vehicles Utilized by Specialized Formations

The primary users of motor vehicles were transport units responsible for supplying provisions to frontline troops. Their main deliveries included essential goods such as food and ammunition. Regardless of general-purpose transport vehicles, certain arms branches utilized specialized vehicles, including heavy artillery tractors, ambulances, postal vehicles, and communication wagons.

3.1 Pioneers

From 1915 onward, pioneer (engineer) units primarily concentrated on constructing field fortifications and supporting the army's mobility on and behind the battlefield. Although a substantial pontoon bridging capability was maintained, its significant use dwindled after 1916, mainly serving to uphold and manage communication lines. Besides facilitating pontoon bridging, the army's pioneers could establish pontoon ferries and construct various obstacle-crossing facilities as needed.

Pioneer formations were equipped with a limited number of motor vehicles, which could be utilized, among other purposes, for towing steel pontoons. Two types of galvanized pontoons were employed: half pontoons, consisting of separate bow and stern sections, each measuring 4.4 meters in length, utilized by divisional bridging trains; and complete pontoons, 7.9 meters long, were held by corps-level bridging trains. The half pontoons weighed 297 kilograms (bow) and 307 kilograms (stern), while the complete pontoons, held by corps bridging trains, weighed almost 500 kilograms each.

A bridge categorized as standard could support transit weights up to 3,14 tons, with additional reinforcement allowing the passage of vehicles weighing up to approximately five tons. Heavy bridges, utilizing double the number of pontoons of a standard bridge, could accommodate vehicles and loads exceeding five tons, provided they moved across the bridge at speeds not exceeding eight kilometers per hour.

3.2 Motorcycle detachments

The first Motorcycle Detachments (*Kraftradfahrer-Abteilungen*) were established by the German Army in October 1914, with the primary mission of securing areas behind the frontlines. As the war progressed and the need for a more structured approach to motorized transport became evident, a significant reorganization of the motorized troops took place in March 1915. This restructuring placed the *Kraftradfahrer-Abteilungen* under the direct control of the *Etappen-Inspekteure* (Inspectors of the Rear Echelon/Sectors), reflecting the critical role these units played in maintaining communication and logistics in the war zone. As part of this reorganization, the motorcycle detachments were renamed and restructured into *Kraftrad-Abteilungen* and numbered from 1 to 20. These units were subordinated to a Field Army (*Armeetruppe*), marking their integration into the broader military structure and emphasizing their importance in the army's operational framework.

Pioneers
German Pioneers were highly mobile units, attached to frontline infantry divisions. They played a crucial role in supporting offensive operations by clearing obstacles, creating pathways through barbed wire defenses, and establishing temporary bridges to facilitate troop movement. Pioneer formations were equipped with a limited number of motor vehicles, which could be utilized, among other purposes, for towing steel pontoons.
Soldiers of the 12th Pioneer Battalion building a pontoon bridge on Elbe River during pre-war exercises. (AC)

A Prussian transportation column utilizes pontoon ferries supplied by pioneers to cross the Danube River. (AC)

Two types of galvanized pontoons were employed by Pioneers: half pontoons and complete pontoons, 7.9 meters long. Note multicolored camouflage. (AC)

Motorcycles

During the Great War, as opposing armies faced each other across the flatlands of France and Belgium, military motorcycles became commonplace on the battlefield. The bike offered the most effective means of transporting messages, and by the end of the war, the military motorcycle had become the preferred choice over the horse or mule for carrying personnel and light supplies, as well as providing the perfect mount for couriers and despatch riders.

A *Wanderer 4 PS Heeresmodell* motorcycle used in France by the the *VIII.Armee.* (AC)

A staff car and motorcycle from an unknown motorized detachment. (AC)

Motorcycles

A group of motorcyclists at the railway station in Avesnes 1915. (AC)

Starting in September 1914, *Kraftradfahr-Abteilungen* (Motorcyclist Detachments) were established and utilized to convey orders and reports between the headquarters of higher levels of command situated at the rear of the front lines. Motorcycle dispatch riders were particularly favored in areas with passable roads, allowing them to navigate around potholes, obstacles, and slow-moving traffic. The motor-drivers wore, especially during wintertime, leather tunics, trousers, overcoats and caps. The leather garment offered much better protection against weather conditions compared to the cloth equivalent.

Rare images taken in the summer of 1915 portray motorcyclists of the 8th Motorcyclist Detachment engaging in a combat reconnaissance exercise. (AC)

Initially, the German military had envisioned a combat role for these motorcycle units, sending armed motorcycles on patrols into enemy territory. However, this concept was quickly abandoned as the battlefield landscape transformed into a treacherous moonscape of artillery craters, making it nearly impossible for motorcycles to operate effectively. Instead, the role of German motorcyclists evolved over time, with the majority being used for dispatch rider duties. Their ability to navigate small roads, bypass traffic jams, and travel faster than many other transport options of the time made motorcycles invaluable for delivering messages and orders swiftly across the front.

In addition to despatch duties, motorcycles were also utilized for scouting road conditions ahead of truck columns, providing critical information on the state of routes and potential hazards. Moreover, they served as emergency transport for vital supplies, such as medical equipment, when other vehicles were unavailable or unable to reach the required location.

As with other motorized formations, the *Kraftradfahrer-Abteilungen* initially relied heavily on vehicles impressed from civilian stocks, including those found in occupied territories like Belgium. Despite the relatively large number of motorcycles in Germany in 1914—approximately 22,000—many of these were not suitable for military service. Consequently, the actual number of motorcycles impressed into the army by August 1915 was only about 1,700. To address this shortfall, the German military procured additional motorcycles, and from 1915 to 1918, a total of 7,572 motorcycles were delivered to the army, all of which were solo machines. Of these, around 4,500 were manufactured by Wanderer, with the remainder primarily produced by NSU, the second-largest motorcycle manufacturer in Germany at the time.

The constant demand for reliable transport, coupled with the harsh conditions of the battlefield, meant that the available motorcycles were often overworked and difficult to maintain, leading to persistent shortages and challenges in keeping the motorcycle detachments fully operational.

Despite all the efforts, motorcycles, like other motor vehicles, remained in short supply throughout the entire war.

3.3 Signal service

The military significance of signaling as a communication method had been acknowledged in the Imperial Army long before the onset of the First World War. By January 1917, its importance was deemed significant enough to warrant the organization of signal troops into distinct corps overseen by a Director of Signals. In July 1917, the signal corps troops underwent another reorganization, adopting the new title of *Nachrichtentruppen*. Their responsibilities were broadened to encompass the control of various communication systems, including telephones, telegraphs, visual and sound signalling, message-carrying projectiles, carrier dogs, pigeons, and more. This newly established military branch also received a limited number of vehicles to transport specialized equipment, animals (e.g. pigeons) and additional staff.

Signal Service
During the First World War, the German military utilized a portable field telephone known as the *Feldfernsprecher*. Detachments responsible for laying cables and overseeing telephone equipment were termed *Fernsprech Abteilungen*. (Photo: Alamy)

The Signal Corps adapted to its needs mostly light lorries, replacing the load box with a specialized box body made of wood panels. Such vehicles could carry wireless, field telephone, field telegraph, or field wire equipment inside. However, larger telescopic radio masts could not be carried inside the box body and were too heavy to be lifted onto roofs, so passenger cars were converted into radio mast carriers (*Funkmastwagen*).

Motor vehicles were primarily utilized for transporting heavy radio equipment, while passenger cars served as staff vehicles at officers' disposal. (AC)

A staff car (likely Mercedes) of the *Fernschprech Abt* . from *the II.Armee*. The photo was taken on the Western Front in 1917. Many staff cars used by signal detachments were converted into *Funkmastwagen* (radio mast carriers). (AC)

Signal Service
The radio mast carrier (*Funkmast Fahrzeug),* was a specialized vehicle designed to facilitate long-range wireless communication. The vehicle's mast could be extended to significant heights, providing better line-of-sight for radio transmissions and overcoming obstacles that might obstruct signals, such as terrain features or buildings. This capability was particularly valuable when traditional ground-based antennae were insufficient to establish reliable communication links. (AC)

Funkmast Fahrzeug of the 34th Field Flier Detachment from the *V.Armee*, Cunel near Verdun 1915. *FAA* units were primarily tasked with observation, necessitating a direct radio link with the Army Headquarters for rapid post-mission reporting. (AC)

A staff car from the 20th Telephone Detachment from the *XV.Armee*. The photo was taken in Romanian Transylvania in 1916. (AC)

3.4 Medical transport

The German Army Medical Service comprised a corps of medical officers (*Sanitäts Offizier Korps*), medical rank and file in the field (*Sanitätsmannschaft*), and the hospital orderlies known as *Militärkrankenwärter*. Additionally, there were regimental stretcher-bearers and ambulance personnel in regular establishments. Stretcher-bearers, classified as non-combatants, identified themselves with red cross armbands.

Wounded soldiers who couldn't be treated at the front-line medical aid post were transported to the dressing station or field hospital, usually situated around 10 kilometers from the front line, where emergency operations took place. For those unable to traverse the distance on foot, a transport service, primarily consisting of horse-drawn ambulance wagons, was provided.

When the First World War erupted, the Imperial German Army was still in the early stages of equipping rear-echelon units with motor ambulances, however first such vehicles were introduced into the service as 1907, however numbers were limited to several dozens in the pre-war period. These vehicles were primarily civilian cars adapted for medical use, rather than purpose-built ambulances designed for the rigors of frontline service. At that time, the army had not yet developed a standardized field ambulance design, and no manufacturer had been tasked with producing a military-specific ambulance model.

With the motor vehicle industry heavily focused on truck production to support the war effort, there were no available resources for the mass production of specialized field ambulances. However, a fortunate outcome emerged from this limitation. Germany's extensive confiscation drives provided a surplus of larger limousines, light trucks, and robust vans that could be repurposed. These vehicles, sturdy in design, became the foundation for creating ambulances. Coachbuilders and local carpenters' workshops across Germany were enlisted to mount ambulance bodies onto these vehicles, adhering to basic army specifications.

This improvisation proved successful, resulting in the production of approximately 4,000 field ambulances throughout the war. By the time the conflict ended in 1918, around 3,100 of these ambulances were still in active service.

One of the key advantages of military motor ambulances was their relatively high top speed of up to 60km/h, which significantly improved the efficiency of transporting the wounded from the battlefield to medical facilities, increasing the chances of saving lives. Additionally, the range provided by motorized transport enabled the army to evacuate more wounded soldiers quickly, allowing them to receive treatment and potentially return to combat.

As of 1 August 1914, each Rear Echelon Medical Depot (*Etappensänitatsdepot*) fielded six motorized ambulances, twelve converted buses and 15 trucks that could be converted to the medical transport vehicles should the need arise.

Each Rear Echelon Medical MV Park (*Etappenkraftwagenpark*) fielded two ambulances and two busses. At this stage there was hardly any equipment unification thus Stationary Medical Vehicle Depots (*Immobile Krankwagen Depots*) and Auxiliary Medical Vehicle Depots (*Krankenwagenhilfsdepots*) had to compose their motor pool with different type of medical service vehicles.

Military ambulances
Motorized military ambulances began to appear alongside horse-drawn vehicles soon after the beginning of the war. Many were make-shift affairs, with large numbers being donated by private individuals or charities based on converted civilian vehicles. The motor vehicles were used mainly to transport wounded from dressing stations (first aid points behind the frontlines to the rear.
Sanitäts Staffel (Medical Squadron) in a Lazaret courtyard at Mericourt on 15 September 1915. The ambulances feature non-standard square red-cross markings. Note the *Daimler Omnibus* with bus trailer serving as *Hilfskrankenwagen.* (AC)

German motor ambulances outside a field dressing station. (IMW)

A Mercedes ambulance belonging to the 1st Medical Service Column. Registration number I-4470 identifies a medical subdivision of the 1st (Field) Army operating in France. (AC)

Military ambulances

The Medical Service, or *Sanitätswesen*, was an independent branch of the German Army that permeated all the other branches of military service. The first ambulances were employed by the Imperial Army as early as 1905, but only after the outbreak of the Great War motorized Sanitary Motor Detachments (*Sanitäts-Kraftwagen-Abteilungen*) were formed at the divisional level, consisting of 8-10 ambulances.

A staff car with a red cross pennant/flag. (AC)

Military ambulance (*Sanitäts Feuerzeug*), from the *VI. Armee*, photographed in Fresnoy, France 1915. (AC)

An ambulance (*Presto* based) marked with *Reichsadler* and red cross roundels. Note that the *JKD 8* stencil on the bonnet indicates that this vehicle was passed to the frontline unit from the Berline-based motor vehicles depot. (AC)

In certain situations, according to pre-war military orders, transport columns operating cargo trucks in the field were authorized to be used for the evacuation of wounded soldiers on their return journey from the frontlines. This directive was born out of the need to maximize the use of available resources, especially during the intense and often chaotic conditions of war when dedicated medical transport might be insufficient or unavailable.

In March 1915, each *Etappenarzt*, a doctor responsible for a rear-sector of an army, was assigned an *Etappen Sanitäts Kraftwagen Abteilung* (Rear Echelon/Sector Medical Motorized Vehicles Detachment or *Et. Sanka* or *ESKA*). The sheer size of these *Abteilungen* made it necessary to break them down into two or three columns *(Kolonne I, II, III)* with five field ambulances (at least on paper) and ten soldiers (five drivers and five co-drivers/medical orderlies) each.

The *Allgemeinen Deutschen Automobil-Korps* was also made available to the *Et. Sanka*, transporting volunteer helpers and wounded individuals as directed by the *Etappenarzt.*

With the reorganisation of the Motorized Troops in December 1916/January 1917, medical service vehicles/detachments were moved to the *Armee* level and were renamed *Sanitäts Kraftwagen Abteilungen (Sanka* or *SKA).* Each *Sanka* was equipped with ten field ambulances, five trucks for medical cargo, staff or patients with ambulance trailers, and a further ten ambulances in reserve. The number of *Sankas* depended on the number of divisions subordinate to a given Army›s command. Under this new structure, most ambulances continued transporting wounded and medical equipment, while some specialized vehicles served as mobile X-rays or disinfection units. As an exception from the rule, some army units also operated their own ambulances, for example the signal detachments (*Nachrichten-Abteilungen).*

The medical corps motor pool also included small or 'micro' cars (*Kleinautos)*, e.g. by *Adler* or *Wanderer*, for use as medical staff cars e.g. for the Army Medical Administration Corps (*Heeres-Sanitatsverwaltung*).

The shortage of ambulances was a persistent challenge throughout the war, much like the difficulties faced with the trucks used by supply units. Civilian vehicle designs, which had been hastily adapted for military use, were never intended to endure the harsh conditions encountered on the often treacherous roads found behind the frontlines. This issue was especially pronounced on the Eastern Front, where infrastructure was poor, and roads were frequently little more than dirt tracks, quickly turning into quagmires in bad weather.

The rugged terrain and severe conditions took a heavy toll on these makeshift ambulances. As a result, breakdowns were frequent, and the need for repairs was relentless. The logistical strain of keeping these vehicles operational was immense, as many were simply not built for the punishing conditions of war.

Compounding these difficulties was the fact that many units had to work with whatever vehicles were available, regardless of their suitability for the task at hand. This resulted in motor pools that were a chaotic mix of different makes and models, each with its own specific maintenance requirements. In some cases, there were no two vehicles from the same manufacturer, nor with the same ambulance body design.

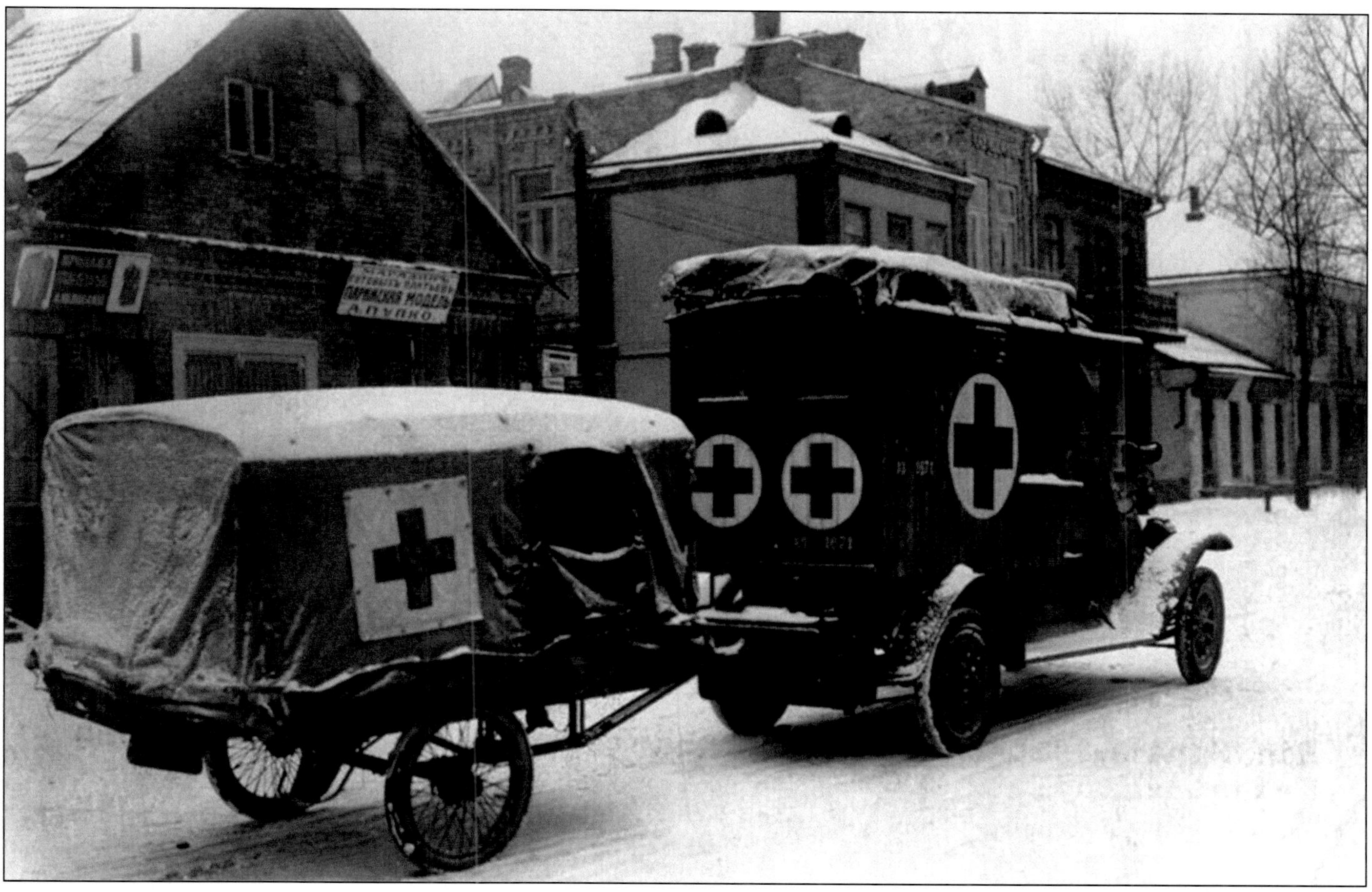

Military ambulances
The Imperial German Army operated a fleet of ambulance road trains made up of a truck towing several two-wheeled trailers. The trailer was well sprung and could accommodate two or three stretchers. An ambulance train from the *XII.Armee* photographed on the Eastern Front, Lithuania, Lida in 1915. (AC)

Two *Mercedes* based ambulances, Type *U1T / UK 12/32 PS*, belonging to the *Etappen-Sanitäts-Kraftfahrzeug-Abteilung, VI.Armee* and *Bayerische-Sanitäts-Kraftfahrzeug-Kolonne*. Both vehicles feature a red cross symbol beneath the respective national coat of arms, the Prussian Imperial eagle and the Bavarian checkerboard. (AC)

Army Air Service

Each *Flieger-Abteilung* or aviation detachment had six *Schleppwagen* or tow trucks for aircraft recovery and transport at its disposal. These trucks facilitated the movement of aircraft between airfields, maintenance facilities, and forward operating bases. This logistical support was vital for repositioning aircraft as tactical and strategic situations evolved.

A truck from the *FFA 32* transporting the remains of a scout aircraft that crashed during a forced landing. (AC)

The prey on the stretcher: Sopwith Camel aircraft Type 2 F.1 built by La Rhone (nine-cylinder radial engine 140hp) towed by an Ansbach truck from the *VI.Armee*. (AC)

A Mathis truck from *Festung* Metz used to transport an early scout aircraft that had crash-landed. Photo taken in 1914-1915. (AC)

Mechanics and repair crews were forced to deal with a bewildering array of parts, tools, and procedures, making it exceedingly difficult to keep the fleet operational. Spare parts were often in short supply, and the technical knowledge required to service a wide variety of vehicle types placed an additional burden on the already overstretched support units. The diversity in vehicle types also meant that repairs took longer and were less efficient, further reducing the availability of ambulances at critical moments.

3.5 Army Air Service

The Imperial German Army started to build its aerial units in October 1913 when the first five aviation battalions were established. At this stage, all aircraft troops formed part of the communication and logistic service. Only on October 8, 1916, the Imperial German Air Service (*Die Fliegertruppen des deutschen Kaiserreiches*) and other branches concerned with air matters such as anti-aircraft, home defense and air intelligence were unified in the *Luftstreitkräfte*.

The first air detachments of the *Luftstreitkräfte*, dedicated to observation, were known as Field Flier Detachments (*Feld Flieger Abteilungen /FAA*) and had an official establishment of six unarmed, two-seat aircraft apiece. Each *FFA* unit was assigned to an army unit in their local area and usually numbered with the same number as the army they were assigned to serve. During 1916, the German Army High Command (*OHL*) reorganized air forces by creating specialist fighter, bomber and reconnaissance units such as single-seat fighter squadrons to counter the Royal Flying Corps and the *French Aviation Militaire*.

All flight units within the German Imperial Air Service were outfitted with lorries designated for the transportation of personnel, disassembled aircraft, canvas hangars, fuel, and spare parts. The expedited transportation of aircraft by lorries held significant importance at the war's onset, given the limited range of aircraft and the occasional inability to reach fully equipped airfields for transfer flights to new deployment areas. Typically, aircraft were initially transported by rail and then transferred by roads to their final assigned airfields. In addition to lorries, each flight unit also possessed a small fleet of staff cars.

3.6 Naval (Marine) motorized units

Lastly, it is necessary to mention that motorized transport formations were aligned with the Imperial marine. The marine transport columns were crucial in providing logistical support to naval bases (harbors) and land-based marine infantry units, with staff cars assigned to HQ units.

The first German marine infantry was established in Stettin (nowadays Szczecin, Poland) on 13 May 1852. The *Marine Korps* initially contributed small contingents to maintain discipline aboard warships and execute limited offensive landing operations. The outbreak of the Great War led to the rapid expansion of marine forces. The *I.* and *II. Seebataillone* were each transformed into a *Marine Regiment* and deployed as the Marine Infantry Brigade at the far northern end of the Western Front on the Flanders coast of Belgium. Drawing upon reservists and conscripts, by the end of 1914, two marine divisions had been established, which, in November 1914, merged to become the new Marine Corps Flanders (*Marine–Korps Flandern*).

Army Air Service
A lorry tows an *Albatros D.V* of *Jasta* (Fighter Squadron) 21 over a country road. France, July 1917. A *Jagdstaffel* (abbreviated to *Jasta*) was a fighter squadron of the German Imperial Air Service during the Great War. (NARA)

A staff car (Opel 35?) tows a *Fokker Dr. I* (198/17) of *Jasta 14*, leaving Bocourt for Masny, preparing for the March Offensive in 1918. The plane is taken from the airfield to the railway loading point. (AC)

A staff car (Mercedes?) from German Army in the East (*Deutsches Besatzungsheer*) somewhere on the Russian Front. In the background a *Halberstadt CL.II* aeroplane. (AC)

Air Service

Drivers of *Jasta 17* waiting in their car in front of the Château Pate in Neuflize, France, Ardennes. (AC)

An Air Service recovery detachment photographed while towing a captured Spad S.XII fighter that had been forced to land in German-occupied territory in northern France in 1917. (AC)

The German Empire and the Ottoman Empire had formed an alliance during the Great War, so it was common for German pilots, planes, and Air Service lorries to be used in the Ottoman Empire's air forces. An Ottoman *Fokker E.III* transported on a German lorry and operated by a German pilot. The German Iron Cross markings were over-painted with Ottoman national insignia. This aircraft served in the 5th Flight Detachment (*Flieger Abteilung 5*), which was a German aviation unit based at Smyrna airfield during April 1916. (AC)

A third division, incorporating hussars and field artillery, was added in early February 1917, elevating the Marine Infantry Corps to a strength of 60,000-70,000 men.

Marine infantry units engaged in battles in 1914 at Antwerp, in 1915 at Ypres, in 1916 on the Somme, in 1917 in Flanders, and in 1918 during the Zeebrugge Raid in April and the German spring offensive.

3.7 Firefighting vehicles

Each major army installation, and certainly all the larger *Etappen-Kraftwagen-Parks* and *Immobiles-Kraftwagen-Depots*, operated their own fire brigades, as German troops could not rely on local firefighting services, particularly in occupied territories. The firefighting units varied in size from squads equipped with a single vehicle to entire firefighting platoons with several vehicles, including fire chief (staff) car, motorized ladders, hose transport and water dispensing monitor/fire engine. The employed vehicles were of commercial designs without any specific technical alterations. While some fire engines might have been transferred from civil units, the majority of new vehicles were directly purchased so as not to draw the emergency lifeblood out of homeland communities.

3.8 Motorised field chapels

Religious solace and spiritual support played a significant role in the Imperial German Army. In rear-echelon areas, churches or larger halls were used by army chaplains for religious services, but closer to the frontlines, services were mostly held in open fields.

Each army division had two military chaplains at the divisional level, one Catholic and one Protestant. Initially, for transport, each chaplain had a coachman and a horse-drawn carriage with two coach horses at his disposal. As motor vehicles became more available, chaplains also used staff cars, limousines, or passenger cars from the division's motor pool. A unique case was the use of *Kapellenwagen* (mobile field chapels), also known as *Kapellenautomobile* (motorized field chapels). In the rare instances these were encountered, a chapel with religious equipment was carried in the rear of a large limousine or field ambulance-type vehicle. These chapels contained religious paintings, symbols, and the necessary tools to conduct either a Catholic or Protestant service. It is assumed that all such vehicles were civilian donations from religious organizations, rather than army purchases, to provide soldiers in the field with a more sophisticated place to worship.vv

Naval Infantry
A staff car from the *Marine Korps Flandern which* was established in 1916 as a joint unit of the German Imperial Navy and the German Army's Marine Brigade. It was responsible for coastal defence and naval operations in the Belgian province of Flanders during the Great War. The unit's main tasks were to defend against the Allied naval blockade and to conduct raids on Allied shipping. (AC)

German Marines were assigned a variety of motor vehicles which were marked with the traditional naval emblems of two crossed anchors topped with the Imperial crown on a white shield, which helped to identify them as a naval unit. (AC)

The *Marine Korps* lorry in the photo has the non-standard, geometric tactical mark of a white rhombus and an individual number (0421) in the left corner of the windscreen translated into the registration number (M 0421). (AC)

Naval Infantry
A *Marine Korps* staff car (possibly a Protos or Opel) bearing license plate M 251 (M for Marine), with a bonnet stencil displaying the tactical markings of the 25th Marine Corps / 2nd Infantry Marine Regiment, temporary service markings of the *JKHD 11* (based in Leipzig but subordinate to *JKD 9* in Breslau; today Wrocław in Poland), and the formation emblem (two crossed anchors) painted on the cabin doors. The photo was taken in March 1916. (AC)

A truck (possibly a Büssing) from an unidentified transport column, providing support to naval infantry, identifiable by the formation emblem painted on the load box. (AC)

A staff car with an NCO crew in the front seats, while the back seats, typically reserved for officers, remain unoccupied. (AC)

4
Moving the Heavy Guns

Artillery in the Imperial German Army was divided into foot (*Fuss*) and field (*Feld*) regiments, the latter were mobile (horse-drawn), equipped in light guns, used to support infantry in the field. Foot artillery, however, manned heavy siege and fortress guns and the larger pieces of field artillery. Initially, most of these heavy guns were horse-drawn, but by the early 20th century, the concept of using steam-powered vehicles to tow heavy artillery gained traction. This led to the establishment of the Steam Vehicle Command (*Dampfwagen-Kommando*) within the Experimental Transport Troops Detachment (*Versuchsabteilung der Verkehrstruppen*).

4.1 Road locomotives

At the dawn of the 20th century, the German Army began exploring more advanced methods of transporting heavy artillery, moving beyond the traditional reliance on horse-drawn systems. In this pursuit, the army procured three steam traction engines from the British company Fowler, which had a branch in the German city of Magdeburg. These engines, named Florence, Malta, and David, were acquired for experimental trials. The positive results from these trials led to further purchases in 1901, including two additional engines from the British companies Thornycroft and Train-Scotte, along with another Fowler engine produced in Magdeburg.

During this period, vehicles powered by internal combustion engines—using liquid fuel rather than the wood or coal required for steam engines—began to attract the attention of the German military. This interest led to the formation of another specialized unit, the Command for Internal Combustion Vehicles (*Kommando für Explosions-Kraftwagen*). The hope was that these modern vehicles would provide a more efficient and versatile alternative to steam engines. However, this initiative quickly encountered significant challenges. The internal combustion vehicles of the time were plagued by weak engine performance and extremely limited off-road capabilities, rendering them ineffective for the heavy demands of artillery transport. As a result, by 1908, the German Army decided to abandon its efforts to develop liquid-fuel-burning artillery tractors altogether, reverting to the traditional use of horse-drawn transport. This decision reflected a conservative mindset that underestimated the importance of modernizing military logistics in the face of emerging technological advances. It wasn't until the outbreak of the Great War in 1914 that the army recognized the critical need to rethink its approach to artillery transport, especially in preparation for the demands of a modern, offensive war. Recognizing the necessity for powerful transport solutions, the German Army eventually placed orders for steam traction engines from domestic manufacturers such as Fowler-Magdeburg, Kemna, and Lanz.

These machines were the only ones with the necessary pulling force to haul the heaviest of German artillery pieces, which often had to be transported in separate loads due to their immense weight. By the summer of 1914, the army had integrated a total of 50 steam traction engines, including steam traction ploughs (*Dampfpflug-Lokomotiven*), steam traction engine road trains (*Dampfstrassenlokomotiven*), and steam-powered trucks (*Dampflastwagen*) into its service.

By 1914, the heavy artillery had at its disposal 3 Steam Tractor Parks (*Dampfpflug-Lokomotiv-Parks*) and 2 Beznol Tractor Columns (*Benzoltraktoren Kolonnen*). The latter unit, consisting of 25 benzol engine-powered tractors, was assigned to naval gun batteries (*Marine-Kanonen-Batterien*), but almost half of those machines were soon found to be defective.

Dampfpflug-Lokomotiv-Parks Nr. 1 and *2* were designated for heavy coastal batteries equipped with heavy 30.5cm mortars (*schwere Küstenmörser*), while *Dampfpflug Nr. 3* was tasked with supporting the 15cm *K.i.S.L.* (*Kanone in Schirmlafette* - L/39.2 gun mounted inside steel plates shielding inspired by Navy designs). These guns had been mounted in fortresses before the war but were relocated to the frontline by steam road locomotives after hostilities broke out. The total weight of this weapon was approximately 20 tons, with 12 tons attributed to the shield alone. The firing rate achievable with this equipment was notably high, reaching up to 9 shots per minute. The recoil recuperation system was minimal, typical of fortress guns of that period, relying mainly on the massive mounting and its static connection to the fortress ground.

Dampfpflug Parks Nr. 1 (Cologne) and *2* (Strasburg) each had 13 steam road locomotives and three small cars, along with 50 personnel or contract employees, including locomotive drivers and stokers, for *Dampfpflug Park Nr. 3* (Metz), 11 steam road locomotives and 1 street locomotive were allocated, along with 24 personnel or contractually obligated civilians serving as locomotive drivers and stokers. Additionally, steam road locomotives were utilized by heavy coastal mortar batteries (*schwere Küstenmörser*

Heavy artillery tractors (road locomotives)
A road locomotive (*Dampf Zugmaschine*) towing a barrel of 21cm *Mörser* that was capable of firing shells over a distance of up to 9.5km. The gun was so large and heavy that it had to be transported in several smaller loads to the assembly area, with the aid of a heavy artillery tractor/road locomotive such as a Daimler or Poel or Lanz. (AC). Note the tactical markings painted on the side box of the 7th Heavy Coast Mortar Battery, 2nd Vehicle.

A 15cm *Feldkanone i.R.* (*i.R. = in Räderlafette*—on wheeled carriage) on the march towed by a road locomotive. (AC)

Batterien) Nos. 2, 3, 5, 7, 9, and 10, each having their own steam locomotives and necessary staff, including locomotive and motor vehicle drivers and stokers.

Following the outbreak of the First World War, the urgent need for heavy artillery transport led the German Army to swiftly expand its fleet of steam-powered vehicles. In the rush to bolster its logistical capabilities, the army confiscated an additional 60 *Dampfpflug-Lokomotiven* and 87 *Dampfstraßenlokomotiven / Dampflastwagen*. These were sourced from a variety of places, including civilian sectors like circuses, where such powerful engines were used to transport heavy equipment. By May 1916, another 43 steam-powered vehicles had been purchased specifically to serve as artillery tractors.

One of the primary issues with steam-powered behemoths was their high visibility on the battlefield. The thick, black smoke produced by burning solid fuels like wood or coal made these vehicles easy targets for enemy forces, particularly in open terrain. Additionally, their fuel consumption was immense, requiring a continuous and extensive supply of solid fuels, which in turn strained the military's already overburdened logistics networks. Their road range was limited, forcing them to remain relatively close to supply depots or railheads where they could be refueled.

A road locomotive of the *Schwere Küsten-Mörser-Batterie Nr. 7 / SKM 7* towing a heavy coastal gun L.12 (*i.R*). Soon after the stalemate commenced on the Western Front surplus naval, coastal defense and fortification guns were taken from forts and naval stores and placed on improvised field carriages. This photo was taken in Vimy, North France, in 1914. (AC)

Heavy artillery tractors (road locomotives)
A road locomotive pulling an ammunition cart and heavy gun through a French town in the summer of 1914. (AC)

Steam-powered artillery tractors based on road locomotives and agricultural tractors, were gradually supplanted by combustion engine tractors. Büssing's first combustion engine attempt to create artillery tractor was very much influenced by its heavy-trucks based on steel-rimmed, spoked, truck tires. The search for an improved version was initiated as early as 1915 and resulted in new model with a large diameter wheels and improved grip. (AC)

The *Motorpflug System Daimler* towing a barrel of 21cm *Mörser*. This type can be recognized by the drum-type fuel tank fitted directly on top of the pendulum front axle. (AC)

Heavy artillery tractors
An ammunition wagon of the *SKM 2* towed by a road locomotive. Creuë, France, 1914. (AC)

A *Motorflug System Daimler* towing a 21cm *Mörser* Until 1917, all heavy guns and tractors were painted in a light grey gloss enamel. Over time, this was replaced by multicolor disruptive camouflage. (AC)

An 80hp Podeus tractor from an unidentified *Fussartillerie Regt,* in travel mode, passing through a French city. Because of its weight the 21cm *Mörser* had to be transported in two loads (barrel separated from the carriage), each hauled by its own tractor. (AC)

Heavy artillery tractors
The first Lanz-Bulldog agricultural tractor, the tricycle benzol-engine *LB* type, was easily identified by the drum-shaped casing for the radiator fan at the front of the engine compartment. Twenty of these tractors were confiscated for army trials in the summer of 1914. The vehicle was operated by a crew of two. The photo was taken in 1915 at the Opladen Motor Park in the Rhine-Wupper District, a key logistical hub serving as a central depot for all wheeled artillery tractors. (AC)

View of an 80hp Lanz tricycle towing the 21cm *Mörser* barrel, covered by a tarpaulin somewhere in France. (AC)

A 15cm *Feldkanone i.R.* on the march towed by an artillery tractor. During the war, the wheels of the 15cm *FK i.R.* were altered for muddy conditions by affixing wheel pads to the circumference to dissipate the ground pressure. (AC)

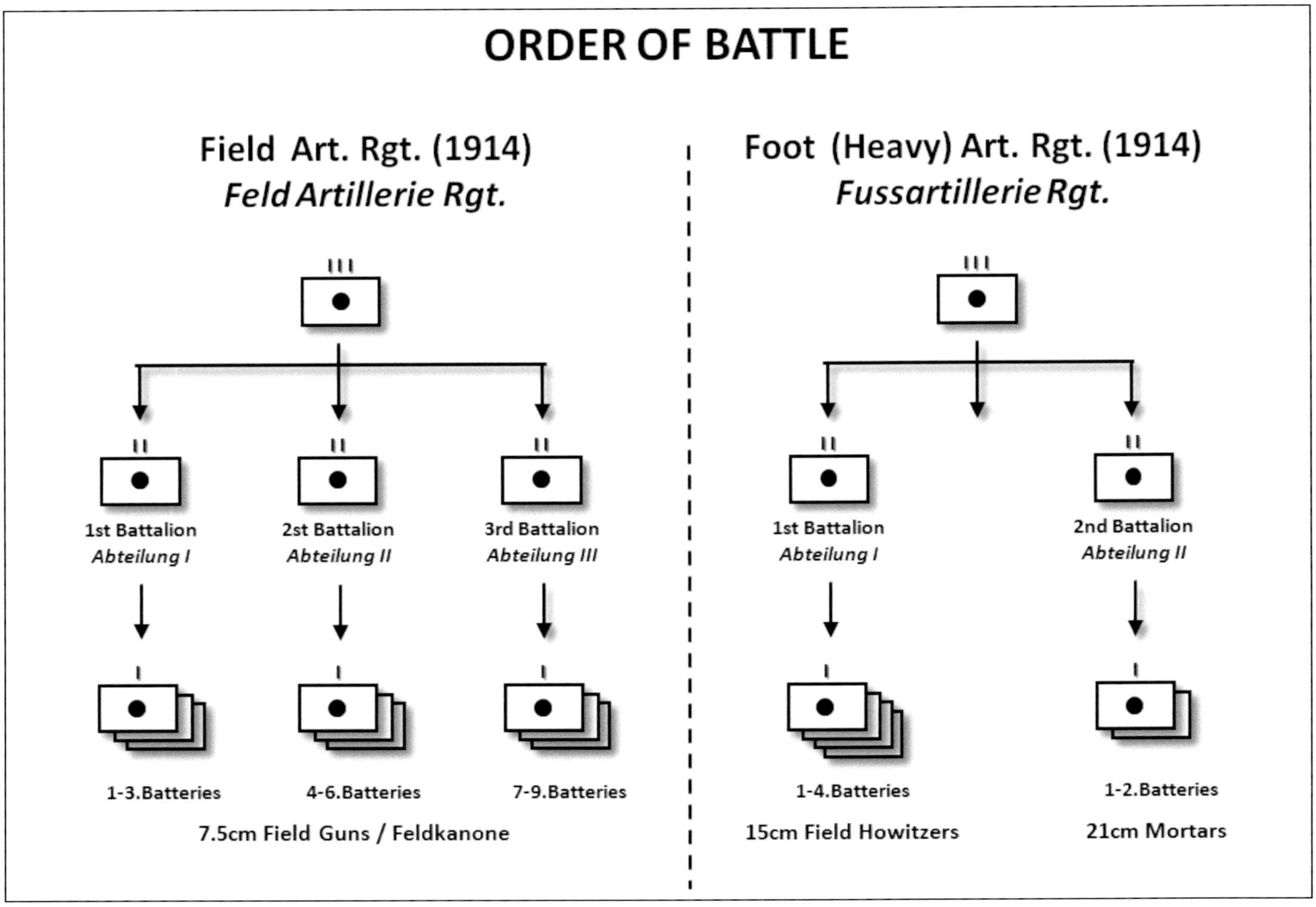

An unidentified *Fussartillerie Regt,* equipped with four 10cm M14 canon and the 21cm mortars, in travel mode, which means the barrel was separated from the carriage. The *Krupp* Kanone 14, accepted into German service in 1914, weighed 2,820 kg. Its tube length was 4.27 m, and it fired a heavy shell out to 12km. It could shoot up to a 45-degree angle and traverse the barrel 6 degrees left or right. (AC)

Heavy artillery tractors
A heavy artillery battery passes through a small town 15km northeast of Laon. The first Büssing tractor pulled the carriage of a 21cm *Mörser* while the tube and accessories had to be towed separately. (AC)

A *Krupp M.16* 15cm Kanone in dapple camouflage. The sheer weight of the gun meant that it had to be deployed in two parts: the barrel and the shield/carriage. It could fire a 52.5kg shell up to 23km. (AC)

A 15cm *Feldkanone SK* L/40 or L/45 from the Dispositional Formation of the High Command during a break in transport. It is packed with the crew's gear, and their belts with bread bags hanging from the barrel. The cannon features an interesting 1918 camouflage pattern. (AC)

Heavy artillery tractors
The *Büssing* tractor was used to tow heavy artillery pieces, such as the 15cm heavy howitzer (*s.F.H. 93*). Photograph taken in front of the *Feld Rekruten Depot 14 R.D.* (*14. Reserve Div.*). (AC)

A Büssing 80/100hp artillery tractor towing two mortar (howitzer) barrels. Based on the registration number (I-2728), this vehicle served with the *I.Armee.* (AC)

A *Lanz* tractor of the Dispositional Formation of the High Command (*Sonder Formationen zur Verfügung der OHL*). All vehicles in a disruptive camouflage pattern similar to the variant used in aircraft (the so-called *Lozenge* pattern) consisting of irregular patches of ocher, green and brown. (AC)

Despite these challenges, most of these steam-powered giants remained in active service throughout the war, from 1914 to 1918. Their continued use was largely due to the fact that they possessed a range of pulling force that could not be easily matched by the more modern 100-horsepower internal combustion artillery tractors, which were still in limited supply and often not as powerful.

4.2 From steam to benzene

The German army's focus on developing heavy and super-heavy, longer-range guns presented a challenge due to the increased weight that made traditional horse teams inefficient for towing these weapons. Even

The movement of such guns posed a great challenge even the barrel and gun carriage were transported as separate loads. This challenge was particularly significant for the 42cm howitzer (*M-Gerät/Dicke Bertha*) due to its immense weight. The howitzer had to be disassembled and loaded onto five separate wheeled transport wagons, each weighing between 16 and 20 tons. With this kind of arrangement, it was thought that a motorized tractor would be the only viable option despite its lack of off-road mobility. Still, the initial reluctance towards mechanical traction was attributed to several factors, including the resistance to technical progress from ageing military leaders, frequent technical failures of early petrol or steam-powered tractors, and the inadequacy of narrow roads for large motor vehicles.

The negative perception of mechanized traction resulted in a limited acquisition of heavy tractors for heavy artillery before 1914. Even when the war broke out, the Evaluation Commission for Transport Technology (*VPK*), as already mentioned, purchased only 60 steam plough engines and 67 steam road engines from civilian firms, with an additional 43 before May 1916.

After the first combat trials of heavy motor tractors in 1915, the report concluded that horses were more effective and reliable in challenging terrain than steam-powered tractors. This was evidenced by the early tractors towing ex-naval 15cm *Schnellfeuerkanone in Raderlafette*, requiring four hours to cover 12 kilometers on a firm straight road and 14 hours for 10 kilometers on a muddy track.

The initial gasoline-powered tractors were produced by firms such as Podeus, Poehl, Sendling, Arator, and Ilsenburg. Among them, the 80 PS (*Pferdestarke* or horsepower) Podeus was deemed the most suitable for moving siege guns.

The perception of motorized tractors improved with the introduction of vehicles powered by benzene. However, initially, the high number of breakdowns of those vehicles disappointed both the *VPK* and Artillery Test Commission (*APK*). Steam traction was briefly reconsidered, but by the end of 1914, it had been definitively declined.

While seeking the optimal vehicle type for towing heavy artillery, German military experts recognized the significant challenge posed by the immense weight of heavy guns, even when disassembled into multiple parts. This problem necessitated an innovative solution for distributing the weight more effectively to prevent guns from sinking into soft ground or becoming immobile.

Heavy artillery tractors
A right side view of the Podeus 80hp artillery tractor based on the *Motorpflug II* (motor plough). The total number of this type delivered in 1916 to the Imperial Army is estimated at 20. (AC)

A left-side view of a late-war Podeus tractor. Note the individual tactical number (3) and the Imperial eagle, identifying the vehicle as belonging to the Prussian Army. (AC)

An artillery tractor (possibly Henschel produced) towing a 15 cm *Kanone 16* heavy field gun which was handed over to the Allies in accordance with the Armistice terms out of an ordnance park near Cologne on 5 April 1919. (NARA)

Load Distribution System by Brauer
The towing speed of an artillery tractor with its associated load distribution system (*Lastenverteilergeräte / LVG)* was between 10 and 16km/h. The connection between the tractor and trailer was made via a pivoting mount located between the rear wheels of the tractor. A rear trailer (*Hinlerwagen*) was used to carry a brake operator who assisted in navigating the tractor-trailer combination through tight turns.
A Büssing 80hp artillery tractor, equipped with a *LVG* 21cm *Mörser*. The photo was taken in France, in 1916. (AC)

An artillery tractor and 21cm *Mörser* M.10/16. Photo taken in a village in the Argonne region, France, April 1918. Note the branch of service badge (two crossed cannons) painted on the *Hinterwagen* used by some foot (heavy) artillery regiments. (NARA)

A *Daimler* tractor with tactical markings of Bay Fs.Art.K.P.3 (*Bayerishe Fussartillerie Kraftzugpark, III Armee*), vehicle No. 7 (W7 / *Wagen* 7). The tractor is uniformly painted with Feldgrau. Pas-de-Calais, France 1916. This model is so rare that only a few photos exist of it. (AC)

In March 1915, a breakthrough came when Engineer Brauer proposed a novel load-distributing system, known as the *Lastenverteilergerät / LVG*. Brauer's invention was specifically designed to address the weight distribution issues associated with heavy guns, such as the 21cm *Mörser* M.10/16. His system ingeniously reduced the ground pressure exerted by the heavy artillery by suspending the gun between a tractor and a specialized semitrailer. This setup allowed the load to be more evenly distributed across a greater surface area, significantly improving the mobility of the artillery on unpaved roads and reducing the risk of the vehicle and its load becoming bogged down. The *APK* quickly recognized the potential of Brauer's invention and approved its development. The responsibility for manufacturing the *Lastenverteilergerät* was assigned to the Rheinmetall company, a leading German arms manufacturer, which ensured that the system would be produced to the high standards required for military use, and it soon became an integral part of the German Army's artillery transport strategy.

By the end of 1915, there was a consensus that motor traction was necessary for all guns of the heavy artillery (*Fussartillerie*), not just the super-heavy guns. This decision resulted in more Brauer load-distributors being ordered for the 13cm guns and the new 15cm guns *Kanone* K 16. Initially, only individual batteries were equipped with cargo trucks for traction purposes, but in 1916, the War Ministry pushed for developing more powerful motorized artillery tractors.

As the number of heavy guns increased, the standard army trucks with 35 horsepower proved insufficient for these loads. Consequently, the *APK* demanded new artillery tractors with a power range between 60 and 80 horsepower, which were subsequently developed by the industry.

On 13 July 1916, the *APK* ordered forty 100hp tractors for the 42cm *M-Geräte*, which had been successfully employed against Belgian forts, particularly at Liège, during the first months of the war. Additionally, sixty tractors with 80hp for the 15cm *Kanone* K 16 were ordered.

In November 1916, the *APK* requested a special truck for ammunition transport, ordering 200 for the year 1917.

Krupp and *Daimler* independently designed a new tractor for the 15cm *Kanone* (or any other 5-ton artillery piece), resulting in the *Krupp-Daimler K.D.I Artilleriezugmaschine*, or the *K.D. I* artillery tractor. Equipped with cast-steel wheels running on steel rims with wood inlays for ‹spring,› these wheels could only achieve limited speeds (12km/h) and tended to slide on roads, causing damage to both themselves and the vehicles. The *K.D. I* could use extra pedrails/wheel belts (*Radeürteln*) on the wheel rims for lower ground pressure when off-road. Due to vibrations, the frame and cardan shaft suffered, necessitating the reconversion of the rear axles to the old chain drive system.

Completed in 1916, the *K.D. I* underwent testing on training ranges and was ready for deployment to the troops in 1917. By the war›s end, an order for 1,070 *K.D. I* was placed, intended for pulling the 15cm K 16 and anti-aircraft guns (8.0cm / 8.8cm), as well as some for the 17cm L/40 ex-naval gun, with 981 delivered by November 1918.

On 24 November, 1916, *Kriegsministerium* laid down the official designations of all military motor vehicles:

- *Artillerie-Kraftschlepper*, artillery tractor, 80hp, with load-distributor for 15cm guns and 21cm mortars.
- *Artillerie-Kraftzugmaschine*, artillery prime mover with 100hp for pulling super-heavy guns and 15cm *KiSL*

Super-heavy lorries / artillery prime movers
A *Krupp-Daimler K.D. I* towing a 15cm K 16 cannon main body. The barrel was separated and travelled on a special carriage, also towed by a *K.D. K.D. I's* were the first four-wheel-drive Prussian artillery tractors built in a larger series which had a base price was set at 59,000 marks. *I.* (AC)

A *K.D. I* lorries from the *VII.Armee* during the transport break. Note a carriage for a 42cm *Krupp* mortar (M.1916) behind the vehicles. (AC)

A late-war variant of *K.D. I* from the *IV.Armee* towing a barrel carriage. (AC)

Heavy artillery ammunition carriers (Above and top next page)

In November 1917, the Supreme Army Command issued a request to prioritize all artillery motor vehicles and other motor vehicles under Class I for production. Consequently, orders were placed for heavy artillery ammunition trucks from Büssing and Horch. The exact quantity of these heavy vehicles remains uncertain, with sources varying from 380 to 460 units. However, the actual number of delivered vehicles was approximately 330.

Based on frontline experiences summarized in 1918, the Büssing (*Artillerie-Munitionsschlepper, abbreviated* as *Art.Mun.Kr. 55PS*) was deemed underperforming, often necessitating replacement by heavy transport lorries in the field. While it exhibited relatively satisfactory performance on paved roads, its off-road capabilities were notably deficient. In contrast, the Horch artillery ammunition tractor was considered field-ready.

Büssing 55PS at factory yard 2 (above), and in the field (top next page). (AC)

Büssing 55PS abandoned near Oberkall, Germany, December 1918. (NARA)

- *Artillerie-Kraftzugmaschine*, artillery prime mover with 100hp, for medium guns, especially the *Krupp* version of the 15cm *Kanone* K 16.
- *Dampfzugmaschine*, artillery steam engine tractor, with 80hp, for 15cm guns in shield carriages and heavy coastal mortars.

By the end of 1916, the stock of artillery tractors consisted of: 380 *Kraftschlepper*, 314 *Kraftzugmaschinen*, and 70 *Dampfzugmaschinen*. From May 1917 until 30 October 1918, Krupp delivered 537 artillery traction engines K.D. I, Lanz delivered 97, Deutz 40, and *Podeus* 20 *Kraftzugmaschinen*.

The enhanced artillery tractors, with increased power, were primarily manufactured by Büssing, Dürkopp, and Lanz, with a smaller contribution from Podeus. While the early models from 1912-1914 clearly showcased their agricultural origins, the mid-war designs were specifically adapted for military use. They featured water-cooled benzol engines and large rear wheels akin to those found on agrarian equipment, providing the necessary traction. Weighing between 5-6.5 tons, the *Kraftzugmaschinen* could effectively tow even the heaviest guns.

For off-road movement, tractors were often equipped with *Radeürteln*. On well-maintained roads, the tractors could achieve speeds of 5-7km/h, and only half of that speed off-road.

The new tractors were initially assigned to the 42cm *M-Gerät* batteries, but by mid-1918, all mobile siege batteries were equipped with a few of those new vehicles.

In addition, at the beginning of 1916, a foot/heavy artillery parks (*Fussartillerie-Park*) were established for each *Armee*, as a support for the motorized *Fussartillery Bataillons*, which consisted of nine lorries for transporting small parts, tools, and supplies. Each *Armee* also received a *Fussartillerie-Munitions-Kolonne* to transport ammunition for the heavy batteries. In 1916 *Fussartillerie-Kraftzug-Parks* became *Armee-Fussartillerie-Kraftzug-Parks* and were increased to 10 vehicles.

Later in 1917, further and stronger artillery prime movers (*Zugmaschinen*), the *Z II* and *Z III*, were developed by *Daimler*, again without asking the military, and only according to *Krupp's* demands that insisted that they had a contract guaranteeing them the sole authority on such vehicles for the heavy artillery.

At the beginning of 1918, the army announced its switch from 80hp to preferably 100hp for heavy artillery tractors, placing orders for such vehicles, among others, with Dürkopp (175 pieces out of which only 91 were delivered), Lanz (210 vs. 97 delivered) and Podeus (20 delivered). The actual production was limited due to shortages in supply materials. Altogether, at the end of October 1918, the artillery had ordered 3,049 tractors, received 2,078, and was waiting for another 1,034. Among the delivered artillery tractors were: 388 tractors (80PS or *PferdStarke* equal to horsepower), 16 tractors (80PS powered), and 1027 tractors (100PS powered). *Krupp* was developing more powerful traction engines (e.g., *K.D. II*) in 1918, but they were not delivered before the armistice.

Considering the starting level in 1914, the number of motor artillery tractors increased significantly, but they were still much smaller than in the case of the Entente forces. At the end of the war, the French provided motor thrust to some 900 heavy artillery pieces, the British to all 152mm guns and above, the Americans to 155mm guns and howitzers, while the Germans only for 441 heavy guns, organized in 217 batteries.

Heavy artillery ammunition carriers

A Büssing artillery tractor towing a heavy 15cm K 16 gun as it passes through the Belgian/Flemish town of De Voerman, marked with the distinct tactical number 3704. It's noteworthy that all *Büssing Art.Mun.Kr. 55PS* were designated with four-digit numbers, commencing from 37. (AC)

A *Horch Artillerie-Munitionsschlepper*, undergoing field acceptance trials. (AC)

Given that only 150 Horch artillery ammunition tractors were supplied to the Prussian army, photographs of these heavy machines are exceedingly rare. The design of the *Horch* was a mix of heavy lorry (front), artillery tractor (rear wheels) and agricultural tractor (front wheels). (AC)

Field gun towing vehicles
As the war progressed, motorized vehicles became increasingly common for transporting field guns. Heavy tractors were used as *train gun movers*, while lorries were converted into makeshift self-propelled guns by temporarily mounting field cannons on trucks.
A Büssing artillery tractor instead of towing a 21cm *Mörser*, tows two 7.7cm *FK 96* field guns. (AC)

A *Büssing* is pulling an unusual combination: a 21cm *Mörser* (howitzer) barrel typically employed by heavy artillery regiments alongside a partially damaged 7.7cm field gun used by field artillery regiments. It appears to be a recovery team tasked with transporting damaged equipment to a gunsmith workshop. (AC)

A Büssing tractor towing a 7.7cm *FK 96* field guns. in front of military barracks of the 14th Reserve Div. of the VII. Corps, which recruited primarily in the province of Rhine-Westphalia. (AC)

Artillery tractors delivered to the Imperial Army between 1914-1918 (estimate)

Type	PS (1)	Manufacturers	Ordered	Delivered	Undeliv.
Dampfzugmaschine / Artillery Steam Engine Tractor (2)		Various	190		190
Artillerie-Kraftschlepper Artillery Tractor	80	*Büssing*	120	109	11
		Benz	105	105	-
		Dürkopp	175	91	84
		Pöhl	84	83	1
Artillerie-Kraftzugmaschine Artillery Prime Mover	80	*Bothe*	72	16	VG
	100	*Krupp-Daimler K.D. I*	1070	855	215
		Lanz	210	97	113
		Deutz	48	40	8
		Podeus	30	20	10
		Hazet	30	14	16
		Komnick	10	1	VG
Artillerie-Kraftprotzen Artiller Tractor		*Benz*	100		100
		Dürkopp	3		3
		Horch	3		3
		Lanz	3		3
		Magirus	3		3
		Imperator Werke	10		10
		NAG	3		3
Artillerie-Zugmaschinen für Flak / Anti-Aircraft Art. Mover	100	*Krupp-Daimler K.D. I*	450	274	176
		Ehrhardt	140	39	101
Artillerie-Munitionsschlepper Artillery Ammunition Tractor	55	*Büssing*	180	180	-
		Horch	200	154	46

1) PS or PferdStarke is the metric measure of horsepower equal to 98.6% of one horsepower, (2) *Dampfpfluglokomotiven* (steam plow locomotives) – 60, *Dampfstrassenlokomotiven & Dampflastwagen* (steam road locomotives & steam trucks, private confiscated) – 87, *Dampffahrzeuge* (steam vehicles) – 42, VG - contract terminated

4.3 Field artillery motorization

The German field artillery commenced the war with approximately 7,000 field guns (mainly 7.7cm caliber) and about 1,300 light field howitzers (9.0 to 10cm caliber), providing the German army with firepower superiority. Unfortunately, Imperial doctrine was not adept at fully exploiting this firepower. Until the outbreak of the war, many generals insisted that the field artillery closely follow the attacking infantry off-road for as long as possible, ideally penetrating enemy lines before firing from open emplacements at short distances. As a result, the field artillery training predominantly focused on maneuvering the guns with horses; peacetime exercises primarily involved transitioning batteries between firing positions, with the regiment commander recording the time using a stopwatch.

This emphasis on mobility led to the development of the new field gun, introduced in 1904 as the *Feldkanone 96* or in short *FK 96* (7.7cm), which had to be both lightweight and mobile. This approach proved effective only during the initial month of the Great War until the Battle of the Marne, where the German advance was halted. From that point onward, the nature of the war shifted from one of movement to one of static positions. Consequently, artillery on both sides began firing from concealed, stationary positions. This shift in the war dynamics necessitated the development of new guns with longer ranges and greater effectiveness.

Field guns transport
A rare photo of a Büssing lorry towing a field gun somewhere on the Western Front in 1917. While at the outbreak of the Great War, a career in the artillery was viewed as a less prestigious posting, by the end of the war, the artillery proved to be the most important arm of the army. (AC)

A makeshift mobile equipped with a *FK* 04 10cm on a 4-ton Büssing truck., during field exercises. (AC)

A Württemberg Army truck, distinguished by the royal coat of arms adorning the driver's cabin doors, employed as a gun carrier by a field artillery battery. This method of transporting artillery was exclusively deployed by a handful of units mobilized to safeguard especially vulnerable sectors of the front line. (AC)

Field guns transport
The *Büssing Type IV*, with a payload of 4 tons, was used from 1918 onwards to move the field guns. The most prominent external feature of this vehicle was the simplified design of the engine compartment side covers, which were made of a single piece of sheet metal. Also, note the no-longer-fitted upper headlights and the full-steel rear wheels, including running surfaces. (AC)

A *Büssing* Type V, 5 tones lorry, with a 7.7cm *FK 96 n.A.* The photo was taken probably on the Eastern Front in 1918. (AC)
The conversion of trucks to gun-carriers included shortening the cargo bay side panels and removing the foldable soft-top of the cab to handle the gun as well as fitting a radiator brush guard.

A *Büssing* lorry with a 7.7cm *FK 96 n.A.* The photo was taken in the West in 1918. Note that the vehicle is marked with service of the *JKD 1* (*Immobile-Kraftwagen-Depot Nr. 1*) in Düsseldorf. (AC)

The importance of mobility in field artillery diminished, yet even in these units, horses were gradually supplanted by motorized transport. However, this transition was confined to a select number of artillery regiments, which also incorporated dedicated *Kraftwagen-Staffeln*.

Towards the war's end, various truck types carrying field artillery guns were employed as rapid deployment forces of the *Heeres-Reserve* (reserve of the Land Forces) to address emerging hotspots. These formations were typically assigned to Army Headquarters as highly mobile reserves.

With the aim to standardize transport for light and medium artillery, the three firms of Magirus, Dürkopp, and Büssing had submitted designs of four-wheel drives, while Daimler, Lanz, and Benz vehicles had tracks. The winning Magirus model, boasting 70hp and a winch for self-recovery in case of being stuck, was designated as the *Kraftprotze 1 (KP 1)* or the Power Limber 1, but it was introduced only in the middle of 1918.

Field guns transport
A *Mannesmann Mulag* lorry from the *Armee Abt. B., Kanone-Kraftwagen-Kolonne 4.* Note the service stencil painted on the front of the load box (Trgf 4.0t or Trgf 4.5t, which stands for *Tragfähigkeit* / carrying capacity). This vehicle was photographed in Macedonia (Prilep) in December 1916. (NARA)

A Büssing lorry, loaded with a field artillery gun from an unidentified *AKK*, was used as a rapid deployment force of the *Heeres-Reserve* (reserve of the Land Forces), France 1917. Note unknown tactical markings – the vertical white bar on the load box. (NARA)

A *Büssing* IIIA truck of the *Armee-Kraftwagen-Kolonne 53*, loaded with a field artillery gun. The lorry is marked with the *JKD 8* service stencil (*Immobile-Kraftwagen-Depot 8*, Berlin-based), the *Reichsadler*, an unidentified triangle emblem (2nd Battery symbol?), and an individual vehicle number (6). It was spotted in Morhange (Mörchingen), France, in 1918. (AC)

Light load artillery tractor (above and bottom previous page)
The *Kraftprotze*, manufactured by the *Magirus* company, boasted a 70hp Otto engine of their own design. Sporting four-wheel drive with a locking differential in the transfer case, as well as differential locks in each axle, all individually switchable, its rear axle was pendulum-mounted. Iron-rimmed wheels, affixed with diagonal lugs, were equipped with radial steel grips extendable from tire slots via spindles while in motion, each spindle featuring a small bevel gear driven by a central large bevel gear pair. To aid steering in rugged terrain, the steering column's worm movement featured two selectable reductions. With a winch positioned at the vehicle's bottom center, steep slopes could be traversed, and the vehicle could free itself from challenging landscapes. Dubbed KP1, this vehicle was finalized in mid-1918 but arrived too late to see any frontline action.
Megirius Kraftprotze at the factory yard. (AC)

Appendix

Development Timeline of Selected German Motorized Vehicles (1914-1918)

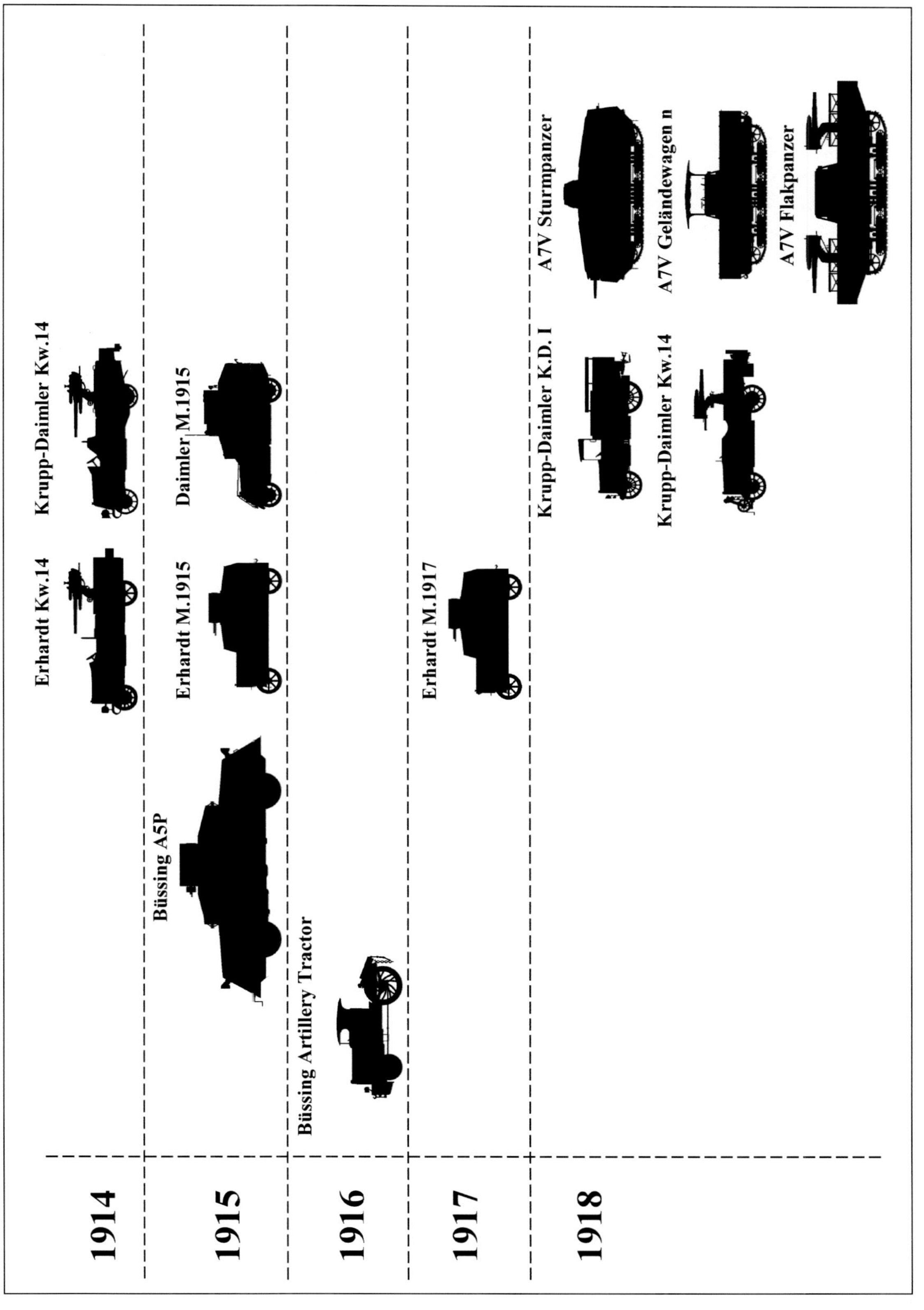

Bibliography

Printed books

Johannes Denecke, *Tarnanstriche des deutschen Heeres 1914 bis heute* (Bernard & Graefe, 2001)
D.S.V. Fosten & R.J. Marrion, *The German Army 1914-18,* Osprey MAA80 (Osprey Publishing, 1978)
Andreas Herzfeld, *Militärische Abkürzungen an Kraftfahrzeugen im 1. Weltkrieg: Ein Wörterbuch* (Flaggenkunde, 2019)
Max Hundleby & Rainer Strasheim, *Sturmpanzer: The German A7V Tank and the Captured British Mark IV Tanks of World War* (G T Foulis & Co Ltd, 1990)
Herbert Jager, *German Artillery of World War One* (Crowood Press, 2001)
Stanislav Kirilec, *Avtomobili-zenitki Pervoi mirovoi voiny* (Jauza, 2021)
Fred Koch, *Beutepanzer im Ersten Weltkrieg* (Podzung Pallas, 1994)
Jürgen Kraus, *Handbuch der Verbände und Truppen des deutschen Heeres 1914–1918, Kraftfahrtruppen Vols. 1 & 2* (Verlag Militaria, 2023)
Thomas Müller, *Die Bayerische Sturm-Panzer-Kraftwagen-Abteilung 13* (Verlag Veit Scherzer, 2013)
Klaus Paprotka, *Taktische Einsätze der Sturmpanzerwagen A7V im Jahre 1918* (Bernard & Graefe Verlag, 2003)
Wolfgang Schneider & Reiner Strasheim, *German Tanks in World War I. The A7V and Early Tank Development* (Schiffer Publishing, 1990)
Rainer Strasheim, *Beute-Tanks - British Tanks in German Service Vol. 1/2, Tankograd WWI Nr 1003/4* (Tankograd Publishing, 2011)
Rainer Strasheim, *Panzer-Kraftwagen - Armoured Cars of the German Army and Freikorps, Tankograd WWI Nr 1007* (Tankograd Publishing, 2013)
Rainer Strasheim & Max Hundleby, *Sturmpanzer, A7V - First of the Panzers, Tankograd WWI Nr 1001* (Tankograd Publishing, 2020)
Nigel Thomas, *The German Army in WWI 1914-15 (I)* MAA394; *1915-17 (II),* Osprey MAA 407; *1917-18 (III),* MAA 419 (Osprey Publishing, 2003-2004)
Carlos de Diego Vaquerizo & Ricardo Recio Cardon , *Deutsche Panzer 1917-1918* (Abteilung 502, 2022)
Carlos de Diego Vaquerizo, *Panzerwaffe Tarnfarben. Camouflage Colours and Organization of the German Armed Forces (1917-1945)* (Abteilung 502, 2021)
Jochen Vollert, *Lastkraftwagen - German Military Trucks Vol. 2, Tankograd WWI Nr 1011* (Tankograd Publishing, 2021)
Jochen Vollert, *Spezialfahrzeuge - German Specialised Motor Vehicles, Tankograd WWI Nr 1012* (Tankograd Publishing, 2022)
Steven J. Zaloga, *German Panzers 1914-1918,* Osprey NV127 (Osprey Publishing, 2006)

Journal articles

Krzysztof Fudalej, 'Cesarska armia niemiecka i motoryzacja podczas Wielkiej Wojny', *Technika Wojskowa Historia 1/2021*, pp. 66-72
Krzysztof Fudalej, 'Skromne początki. Czołgi, obrona przeciwpancerna i armia niemiecka podczas I w.ś.', *Przegląd Historyczno-Wojskowy 2020/1,* pp. 62-100.

Archival Sources

Bundesarchiv - Abteilung Militärarchiv (BArch-MA), N 610/15, N 610/16, N 610/19

Websites

https://www.feldgrau-forum.com/
https://www.flickr.com/photos/drakegoodman/
https://archiv-axel-oskar-mathieu.de/